SONG OF THE OUTCASTS

Aurora Vargas, a Gypsy singer who can dance, too. Photo: Miguel Angel González. Courtesy of the Centro Andaluz de Flamenco

SONG

OF THE

OUTCASTS

An Introduction to Flamenco

by Robin Totton

Amadeus Press
Portland ✦ Cambridge

Printed in Singapore

Published in 2003 by
Amadeus Press (an imprint of Timber Press, Inc.)   Amadeus Press
The Haseltine Building   2 Station Road
133 S.W. Second Avenue, Suite 450   Swavesey
Portland, Oregon 97204 U.S.A.   Cambridge CB4 5QJ, U.K.

Library of Congress Cataloging-in-Publication Data

Totton, Robin.
    Song of the outcasts : an introduction to flamenco / by Robin Totton.
       p.   cm.
    Includes bibliographical references (p.   ) and index.
    ISBN 1-57467-079-4—ISBN 1-57467-080-8 (pbk.)
    1. Flamenco music—History and criticism. 2. Flamenco—History and criticism. I. Title.

ML3712 .T67 2003
781.62'610468–dc21
                                                            2002029919

Para Pepe Guardia
sin el cual . . .

CONTENTS

ACKNOWLEDGMENTS

Many people have helped, but above all three before I had a publisher and three after: José Guardia Rodríguez of Granada gave me endless time and hospitality, taking me through the song forms and round the flamenco locales; Paco el Melchora of Jerez, from my first visit to a *peña*, took me under his wing and has treated me like an adopted son; and when I had no editor, Jay Upton read each chapter and was ruthlessly critical on detail, heartwarmingly encouraging of the whole. Without these three, this book, whatever its failings, would not exist.

Eve Goodman, of Amadeus Press, combines generosity, toughness, and diplomacy to a rare degree; Walter Clark, of the University of Kansas, knows more about Spanish music, classical and folk, than I thought possible, and his detailed suggestions were most helpful; and Barbara Norton edited the text with care and speed.

1

Why? What? Where? Who?

How are you going to be able to talk about Spain after you've actually been there?

HEINRICH HEINE TO THÉOPHILE GAUTIER

Why

There are hundreds of books on flamenco in Spanish, dozens in French, and even one or two in English. But only one, written nearly half a century ago by Donn Pohren, sets out to explain it—to help the rest of us enjoy it more. There are thousands of English-speaking people who see it while in Spain. When Cumbre Flamenca or Corazón Flamenco or Paco Peña's company plays in London it is almost impossible to get a seat. The same was true for Cumbre's predecessors Antonio and Rosario, José Greco, and others. What is more, there is growing interest worldwide both in dance and in ethnic music; and in Spain itself, growing appreciation for flamenco, which is the ethnic music of Andalusia. To fill this gap is one of my reasons for writing this book.

There is another one. If you are unused to classical music and listen to a Mozart piano concerto, you cannot share the depth of enjoyment a devotee finds in it. The same is true for a Gothic cathedral, a ballet, or any other work of art. You don't need to be an expert—a musician, an architect, or a dancer. But you do need either some familiarity or else some pointers as to what is happening and how it works. If you have neither, the Mozart may

Chapter 1

sound, or the ballet look, very pretty at first, but after a few minutes it all begins to seem rather the same, and you begin to wonder what is for supper. Once you have begun to get inside them, though, you wonder how your attention could ever have wandered: the richness and variety increase your enjoyment with every moment and at every hearing.

Another reason for writing this book is that even if many people in many countries enjoy the dance—even appreciate it to some extent—such enjoyment is perforce limited, for I suspect that very few like the song. To most people it sounds less like music than the howling of wolves in the tundra. Yet flamenco is song first and foremost. Both dance and guitar stem from the song and are subservient to it. The dance is certainly ancient. But ever since flamenco became known to the public, which is to say ever since the early nineteenth century, the dancer has interpreted the song. As for the guitar, until quite recently it was there simply, if at all, to give the singer some rhythmic accompaniment. The solo guitar emerged only a few decades ago. To dismiss the song as background noise is comparable to watching *Swan Lake* without either Tchaikovsky's music or the story line.

When I first came to Andalusia, I enjoyed the flamenco, but I wished there were something to explain the differences between the various songs and dances. There wasn't, and since I was an explainer by trade, I decided to learn enough to do the job. I reckoned three months or so should be enough. A year later, I was just beginning to understand it (and I'm still there). A humbler and fractionally wiser man, you might say—but not a sadder one, because I got hooked by a music that goes deep into people's lives, and by people who are friendly, helpful, deeply courteous, and blessed with a genius for enjoying life. It is contagious. Yet at the same time I was pained by the pabulum that is so often offered to tourists.

If you live in Andalusia among flamenco performers and followers, it is soon borne in on you that the real thing bears little relation to the tinselly stuff put on for the tourist trade. The one is usually trivial and often corny.

The other is an ancient art form that gets to people and holds them to such an extent that it becomes a central part of their lives. It has a strong tragic vein that, when tapped by the finest singers, gives the impression of a sort of ancestral memory. To hear Manuel Agujetas sing a *toná* brings to my mind that creepy line of T. S. Eliot: "The backward half-look, over the shoulder, toward the primitive terror." (Have you ever walked through a wood, in the dark, after rain, when the trees are dripping? Without glancing over your shoulder?) And even in its festive forms, a *bulería*, performed *among* flamencos rather than merely *by* them, is an unusual experience, of which the onlookers supplying rhythm and vocal encouragement are as much a part as dancers and singers. Track 6 on the accompanying compact disc will convey the idea. None of this has much to do with the upbeat, two-chord strumming, the twiddling girls, and the silly hats of kitsch flamenco. To show the difference was another aim of mine, one that was urged on me by those who helped me. The tourist venues, known as *tablaos*, give the artists a living, which is good, but they trivialize the art. And I don't believe it need be so: those of you who have seen Manuela Carrasco dance at Sadler's Wells may wonder what on earth she had to do in the tablao in Torremolinos, but it gave her her start in life. You may, with luck, see some fine artists in a tablao, but usually the management insists on easy, upbeat rhythms. Meanwhile, on the big stage, what is done by the best performers, while incomparably better than what you find at the tablao, is still a far cry from what you hear and see when a few flamencos get together over a drink. For staged flamenco is performance first, and expression comes only second.

What? Where? Who?

Flamenco is the music of Andalusia, the southernmost region of Spain. It extends to the southern part of Extremadura and to Murcia. It is also to be found in Madrid and Barcelona—but then so are a million or so Andalusians. However, flamenco is not otherwise Spanish, and the average Spaniard is likely to know no more about it than the rest of us. It is not even the folk music of Andalusia: it is, rather, a mode of expression that transforms such music. The folk songs of Huelva province, for example, were taken up by flamenco singers only a few decades ago, and their transformation is far from complete, while other song forms seem to go back into the mists of time. The question of who originated the style causes endless argument. Certainly the Gypsies are important, but flamenco is not exclusively theirs. They have been largely responsible for its survival, and they like to think it belongs to them. But the Gypsies did not bring their own music to any country they settled in. What they did was adopt the music of that country and bring to it their own particular style of musicality, their strong rhythmic sense, and their tendency to dramatize. They have been its catalysts, but flamenco developed from the melting pot of Andalusia. The country was ruled for nearly eight hundred years by the Moors, a Muslim people, themselves a rich mixture of Arabs, North African Berbers, and others. For nearly all that time they were a tolerant people, accepting in their society Christians—Iberian, Celtic, or Visigothic—as well as descendants of Greek colonists, retired Roman legionaries, the Sephardic Jews (who populated Spain in very large numbers), Tartessians (nobody knows quite who they were), Carthaginians, and the Phoenician people of Cádiz, who were already famous as dancers in Roman times.

After the Christian Reconquest in 1492, the Christian intolerance of the times drove the Moors and Jews out—or underground, beyond the pale, forced to survive in the hills or caves, or else living on the hospitality that Gypsies have always given to those fleeing from the law. By the same token, it drove their music—and the Moors and Jews alike were musically sophisticated peoples—underground. And there it stayed, performed in the privacy of houses or caves, unknown to the world, until the end of the eighteenth century.

This music then began to be heard in taverns and other public places. And from then dates our first information about it. So flamenco *as we know it* started only in the nineteenth century. Telethusa, the girl from Cádiz, danced in ancient Rome to the rhythm of castanets and hand clapping. There is strong evidence that both the song and the dance go back a very long way indeed, back even to primitive man. But we can really know about what has happened only in the last two hundred years. And we know only a little of that, because for most of this period flamenco was largely neglected as low stuff, the music of the common herd, not worth serious attention.

It is indeed the music of the people. To this day, few of its performers can read a note of music: they learn from one another other by listening. The inability to read it is no hindrance to the making of fine music—in our own day the Beatles, at the start of their careers, showed this. And even the Indian ragas, I am told, are handed on by aural tradition. But musical illiteracy also applies, alas, to most of those intellectuals and theorists who have written the two to three hundred books on the subject, books that push theories but explain nothing.

Eighty years ago a singer would have to travel to learn from another. Antonio Chacón wanted to learn the *petenera*, a song form that had almost died out. Eventually he heard of a singer in Seville who knew it. So he went there to ask the man to teach it to him. The old man sang and the young man learned. Meanwhile, outside the door young Arturo Pavón eavesdropped. And the petenera came back to popularity through the fame of Pavón's sister Pastora, La Niña de los Peines, who presumably learned it from Arturo.

With today's CDs, cassettes, and radio—and the increasing prosperity that makes them affordable—songs, styles, and innovations spread more quickly and easily, though flamenco musicians still learn from one another. The Fundación, as it is known, or Centro Andaluz de Flamenco in Jerez, is by no means only used by researchers. Young Gypsy lads, aspiring singers or guitarists, come in to watch videos of their idols and learn from them. It is refreshing to be interrupted by the sound of one of them hitting his desk with excitement and exploding with an "Olé! Que sabe!"—and perhaps the more so if you know that the word *olé* comes directly from the Moorish cry "By Allah!" Thanks to recordings, you hear verses of flamenco song lifted from the Andalusian poets Rafael Albertí and Federico García Lorca. There is a singer who calls himself Fosforito de Láchar because he admires the singing of the great Fosforito to the point of imitating him—necessarily from recordings, since the original has retired. The same applies to guitarists: I have heard in their *falsetas* (the twiddly bits they put in between verses of the song) snatches of Enrique Granados, and even (once) Beethoven. But whether live or through recordings, it remains true that flamencos learn from one another.

It is folk music in the sense that it is of the people, not an art learned as classical music is learned. But the term can be misleading, because it has associations for us that do not apply. For us, folk music is either "pure" and enjoyed by a minority, who tend to preserve its purity and by the same token fossilize it. Or it is popularized, like country music in the United States, and taken over by Nashville, or else taken up by such artists as Joan Baez and Bob Dylan and politicized to create a highly professional protest music in the folk form.

But "folk" meaning "of the people," yes. In the flamenco venues you will come across a sprinkling of lawyers, bankers, and businessmen; but most of the ones that I know are itinerant peanut or prawn vendors, laborers, market workers, factory hands, and such. The word *folk* may also mislead, by conjuring up the image of jolly peasants, albeit dressed in garishly exotic dresses. The people who both perform and *live* flamenco are as riddled as you or I by fax and plastic and computers, supermarkets, school tuition, and carbon monoxide.

Immediately I feel the need to justify the phrase "people who *live* flamenco." A hundred yards up the street from my apartment is a disco that dispenses rock on Friday and Saturday nights. Within a minute or two of its closing, at about two-thirty in the morning, a crowd of young people pours out onto the street, factory workers, secretaries, and students, all chattering and laughing. I imagine this scene is familiar wherever there are discos. What happens next is different. Someone starts to clap a rhythm; others join in; then one of them starts to sing. And what they sing is flamenco—specifically *bulerías*, because this is Jerez, where the bulería was invented. They have danced to rock music for the last three hours; now for the next three they'll sing flamenco. I do not want to suggest a romantic scene; it is a gray and rather grubby street, and when you are trying to sleep at four in the morning, the noise, punctuated by the sound of broken glass, is not romantic. I only want to show that flamenco is essentially not a matter of stage performance, nor does it belong to some fictitious, *Carmen*-ridden past. It is an everyday part of the lives of a lot of the inhabitants of Andalusia. And it is more flourishing now in the beginning of the twenty-first century than it was ten or twenty years ago.

You would not have the same experience all over Andalusia. You could live for months in Granada without hearing any flamenco unless you went to a tourist tablao, or the occasional performance organized by a municipality, or a chanced-on district festival where the song would compete with the noises of the fairground. I mention Granada because that is where I first went to live to gather the experience to write this book. I had to hunt to find flamenco there. It is as alive in Granada as it is elsewhere, but not as a public phenomenon so much as a sort of subculture. This is partly because the Gypsies are flamenco's main torchbearers, and in Granada they are marginalized: they are despised and often even hated by other Granadans, so they keep to themselves. I was lucky to be befriended by a small-town lawyer whom the Gypsies trust and like. Seeing him help me, some of them accepted and befriended me too. Only then did I get to know their private *peñas* (flamenco clubs) in the Albaicín district, whose existence I had never suspected. But flamenco is Andalusian rather than exclusively Gypsy. Every week there were singing competitions, if you knew where to find them, in suburbs, villages, and small towns, all over the province. The atmosphere of these provincial peñas was very much that of the English village pub. So were the customers. Once I stopped trying to hunch down and look inconspicuous (fat chance for a six-foot-tall foreigner!) and began to let myself be sociable, I found not that I was intruding on something that was theirs, but that they were delighted I should share their enthusiasms, and very welcoming. Once again, my point is that flamenco is part—often an important part—of ordinary people's lives. It is not a performance art laid on for a ticket-buying public. Many of the photographs in this book were taken at a wedding, an engagement party, or a party during the May fair, or even simply in the street or at a bar.

The people involved may be singers, dancers, guitarists, or suppliers of rhythm (via clapping, tapping with the knuckles, and nowadays sometimes box drums). But they will also be mothers, fathers, children, friends, relations, and others. They are not mere fans, for they, too, participate. And they are never silent listeners: if they are not taking part in the rhythm or egging the performer on with *jaleo,* their cries of encouragement, they will be eating, drinking, and chatting. There is no such thing as a passive audience.

Flamenco is the opposite of "pure" folk music as I described it here, in that the singer recreates it in his own way at each performance. This is much more than just interpreting it, in the way a singer does with classical or popular song. For this reason they do not have "songs," but song forms, called *palos*—a good word, since it means a suit of cards. These song forms the singer recreates on each occasion in the way he (or she) embroiders on a basic skeleton—melodic or rhythmic—and also by the words. Thus, he doesn't sing a *soleá,* he sings *por soleá*—"in the soleá form." And so, unlike folk music, flamenco is constantly changing, not only with the times, but with each singer, and every time he opens his mouth to sing.

Figure 1. Performance at a wedding. Patricia Ibañez and friends: this was her wedding present to her sister.

Re-creation, then, is one of flamenco's central defining characteristics. A second is that it is a solo art, always—even when several are performing together. There is no such thing as choral flamenco; and in the dance, if you find two dancers doing identical movements, you can be sure that it is not the real thing, but part of today's trend toward modern dance. True flamenco dancers do perform in groups, for they need to earn a living, to put on a show. But while their movements may be synchronized, they won't be carbon copies of one another—in fact, they won't even be symmetrical.

Figure 2. Rehearsal for an engagement, in the grim surroundings of the practice room. The five-year-old at the left was so fascinated, she joined in— and the dancers made room to help her. By the age of eleven, she was already dancing in public.

A third characteristic is that flamenco communicates strong, uninhibited feeling—the flamenco says of singing that affects him, "It speaks to me" (*me dice*). Flamencos do not even think of their art as music in our sense, but of its getting through to one. They are not interested in beautiful sounds or movement; strength and force of expression are paramount. The most admired singers have hoarse voices that at moments sound strangled by the violence of emotion. One of my favorite singers can sing with a lilt, but her voice sounds like a cross between gravel and velvet—flamencos think of it as metallic (*de cobre*). The flamenco guitar has a low action that facilitates the technique of *rasgueado* (the rhythmic thrumming across the strings with the back of the fingers). If this low action sometimes makes the strings jangle harshly on the frets, then so be it. Only in recent years have players started to adopt the techniques and tone of the classical guitarist. The dance, too, conveys force and *pellizco* (bite) rather than grace. A ballet dancer will spin round gracefully and come to a graceful stop; a flamenco dancer will spin round at violent speed and come to a stop so sudden that it astonishes. It should be added, though, that today professionally trained dancers are taking over more and more from the Gypsy dancer of family tradition, and you will see grace combined with force. The financial success of flamenco theater and film is tending to move the art toward a balance of the two aesthetics.

As important a characteristic of flamenco as any of the above, is that it is built on strong and complicated rhythms. What the singer does is too complex to be described briefly here (or perhaps anywhere, since musicians, including the composer Manuel de Falla, have tried and failed to identify their rhythms). But the dance clarifies the point. To the dancer, the soleá has an underlying rhythmic structure, or *compás*, expressed by the so-called twelve-count, where the heavy type represents a strong beat:

1 2 **3** 4 5 **6** **7** 8 9 **10** 11 12

This forms the unit equivalent to our bar. It is repeated throughout and it underpins the dance. You might think of it as a sort of two-bar unit, but I don't think that would be helpful, because even though the guitarist keeps time with this rhythm, starting on count 1, his accents or stresses are not the same as the dancer's. In musical terms, he plays it more like a bar of 6/8 plus one of 3/4 (with an extra accent on the tenth note):

1 2 **3** 4 5 **6** **7** 8 **9** 10 (11 12)

in which the numbers in parentheses represent silent beats. From this stems a cross-rhythm of a complexity and subtlety only suggested here, since the notation leaves out not only the different rhythms and accents of the singer, and of the *palmeros*, who clap rhythms and counterrhythms, but also what the dancer does within the framework of the twelve-count.

If you watch a performance of a soleá and keep this twelve-count in mind, you will see how strictly the dancer conforms to it, even though the dance may look free and improvised. What you almost certainly won't do is actually hear it as a rhythm in the dance, song, or guitar, any more than you would hear the 4/4 time of a symphonic movement as a regular beat of 1–2–3–4, leadenly repeated. The twelve-count underlies the rhythms being created by the dancer—syncopated, dragged, and cross-rhythms—as well as those being created (differently) by the guitarist and the singer. If their stresses coincided, the flamenco would think it boring.

No discussion of flamenco—the song, dance, guitar, or song forms of the next four chapters—is possible without the word *compás*. It means slightly different things, according to context. In Spanish music it means simply the bar or measure and, by extension, the rhythm given by the different sorts of measure: 3/4, 4/4, 6/8, and the like. To the flamenco it also means the rhythmic unit of the song. This may be a twelve-count, such as that of the soleá, which I quote above, and which is the same for the *alegrías* and the *bulerías*; or slightly different ones used for the *siguiriyas* and others; or another unit made up, for example, of two bars of 4/4. *Compás* also means to stick accurately to that unit while making rhythmic variations within it. But to a flamenco, *compás* means something else again, and perhaps none of the above. For it is the foreign student who learns the twelve-count. The flamenco has had it inside him since the cradle—probably since the womb—and might well look blankly at you if you referred to it. His knuckles may mark his singing with something that approaches its accents (thus, with what I represent as vertical strokes in

. . | . . | . | . | . |

for the *soleá*, or

| . | . | . . | . . | .

for the siguiriya). But only the foreigner's lips move to the twelve-count. This, if anything, *prevents* the dance student from getting good compás, for his counting is mental (and therefore intellectual): it deals with time and meter, which are not the same as pulse and rhythm. The compás could be compared to what a jazz musician would refer to as being "in the groove" (which is indeed the meaning of the Andalusian word *soniquete*). This pulse, this internal urge, pushes the flamenco to explode into the dance at what seems, to the foreign student, the "correct" moment, and then enables him to shape it powerfully.

Even as I write this I am aware of how inadequate the words are to convey what happens, and perhaps you don't even need to know, in order to enjoy flamenco song and dance. But I am also aware of how fundamental this compás is to the flamenco. In fact I agree with a (foreign) dancer who feels that the compás lies at the heart of flamenco culture.

I shall try to explain why. It is a culture not based on reason, but one in which emotion and instinct dominate in life and are expressed and fulfilled in art. Historically, the flamenco, whether Gypsy or Andalusian peasant, is the poorest of the poor. He is a slave (to hunger, to the need to find work), while his employer is free to do as he likes. He is (usually) illiterate, with all the confinements that entails. He knows hunger and homelessness, as well as the things that we all know: the pain of bereavement, of failed love, of the treachery of friends. The compás gives him a framework for self-expression, one felt inside him rather than understood. And it is what brings him fulfillment. It is the law that gives him freedom—the freedom to release his feelings while giving them artistic shape. The freedom to be himself, and to hell with the world.

Chapter 1

If this is still true today, with the freedoms that today's prosperity brings, it is precisely because Andalusians—Gypsy or *gachó*—are instinctual and emotional first, and rational only after. They are characterized by spontaneous emotion, uninhibitedly expressed. This characteristic is attenuated by education, but of this the flamenco usually has little. In conversation he may suddenly burst into ferocious argument that seems to you to be heading for a fight, and then just as suddenly revert to calm conversation. Likewise, foreigners visiting the *ferias* marvel at the Andalusian's gift for spontaneous enjoyment. In just this sense, his dance or his song expresses emotion strongly felt. It may be conjured up by emotions that have built up inside him, or by the compás. Either way, it will be a *desahogo*, a release of inner tensions. Otherwise it is nothing, a mere going through the motions for the money.

The foreigner learning to dance or play often fails to understand this. She knows she has a good sense of rhythm (she wouldn't be a dancer else), and she has learned about the twelve-count. So she doesn't realize she does not have compás. And the flamenco, no less often, is too courteous to tell her— or doesn't know how to. There is a culture gap that many fail to cross, perhaps because they don't even realize it is there.

There is more to compás even than this. Each area, each town, sometimes even each parish has its minor variants. Take the bulería, for example. The way they sing and dance it in Jerez, where it was invented, differs from the way others do it: for a start, they break it down into a count of six rather than twelve. There was a revealing example of such slight differences recently when Inés Bacán was singing *por soleá* in London. A young flamenco from the Calle Nueva—the heart of the Gypsy quarter in Jerez—got up and walked out. He said she had no compás. This was the blind arrogance of youth. He was too parochial to realize that she comes from another town, where there are slightly different ways of attacking the soleá, and he did not stop to consider that Inés Bacán was broken-hearted at the death of her

Figure 3. The gift for spontaneous enjoyment: waiting for the bull-ring doors to open.

brother. Her soleá was heart-rending. It was good flamenco. But it wasn't done the way they sing it in *his* street.

So. A form of communication generated by emotion unrelated to intellect; complicated rhythms; an art that is essentially individual, and expresses that individuality; the forceful expression of strong feeling, rather than prettiness of sound and movement; and a musical form that is re-created at each performance: these are the main characteristics of an art that evolved as the

25

Figure 4. Spontaneity:
A wedding guest feels like
singing.

music of outcasts, of people harassed by the law or hounded by the Spanish Inquisition and living outside the pale of society. Not surprising, then, that it is primarily a tragic expression of the human condition. It is never the expression of social protest: in the tragic forms, the words of the song express a personal anguish—a cry of despair in the siguiriya, or stoic resignation in the soleá. (There are *one* singer, El Cabrero, and *one* song form, the *taranta*, that convey an occasional note of social protest.)

Flamenco is tragic—or else, by reaction, festive. There is an obvious parallel—though one misleading if taken too far—with the music of the blacks

Figure 5. Spontaneity:
Mijita Carpio throws
an engagement party;
his mother decides
to join in . . .

Figure 6. . . . and
Grandma wants to sing.

in the United States, especially the early blues and New Orleans jazz: "Nobody Knows the Trouble I've Seen" had its flip side in the wild exuberance of King Oliver's "Funeral in New Orleans."

Music of the outcasts, the downtrodden, the persecuted; and music that is in constant evolution. There is a paradox and a problem here, one that is being much discussed at the moment. For how can such a music evolve (or perhaps even survive) among people who, today, have the means to give their children enough to eat, clean clothing, and even shiny bicycles—people who are bombarded, moreover, with music of all sorts, with television fodder, with international pop, through radio, television, and cassette player; who, if they are successful artists, are under pressure from the recording managers to produce only the upbeat, only what is rhythmically basic and accessible to a mass public?

The following chapters aim to help you get further inside the song and the dance and to look in a bit more detail at these questions.

2

The Song

Every time I hear a Gypsy singing a deep song with all his body and all his soul, I feel he is asking me a question to which I have no answer.

MIKIS THEODORAKIS

Of the four main ingredients of flamenco (song, dance, guitar, and rhythm), the song is the one that fewest people find enjoyable, or even understandable. In the 1840s Richard Ford dismissed it as "the howlings of Tarshish," thereby ascribing it to prehistory. It is unlike any music we are familiar with, either the music itself or the use of the voice to sing it, and anything outside the frame of convention with which we are familiar is likely to sound to us like noise. Even within the frame of classical music you need some familiarity with the composer's language: only a few years ago, when an audience emerged from a concert, you would hear people say that Mozart (or whoever) was fine but they "couldn't understand" Bartók (or whomever). Music is sounds arranged into patterns, and they were familiar with the patterns of Mozart but not those of Bartók, and that, I think is what people mean by "understanding" music. If they don't perceive the pattern, it becomes mere noise. We felt the same about the Indian raga until the 1960s accustomed us to it. For that matter, to a pop fan unfamiliar with classical music, Beethoven would probably sound just like a lot of noise. It is partly a matter of understanding, more often one of familiarity.

Figure 7. Forceful expression: El Bizco de los Camarones sings *por fandango*.

The Song

The aim of this chapter, together with chapter 5 on the song forms, is to offer that small dose of understanding necessary. From then on, the familiarity can come quite quickly. If you have enough interest to want to listen (perhaps because you already like the dance or the guitar), you may well become hooked. I know people who went to Andalusia for the dance and became hooked by the song to the exclusion of all else. The attraction is visceral. The flamenco who first helped me to get inside the song told me: "You'll know when you've started to understand: it'll be the moment when you hear a song, or even just a note, and the hair stands up on your arms." There was some truth in this—but I think it also helped that I had come to perceive the pattern.

The most important thing to realize is that when we listen to a song, what we in other Western lands hear first and foremost is the tune, and we may or may not become aware of harmony or rhythm. When an Andalusian listens to a song, what he hears first and foremost is rhythm, words, and expressive force. To him melody is unimportant, and harmonies are no more than a recent addition to flamenco. We non-flamencos often find that in our music the tune hooks us to the point of making the words unimportant. Not so the Andalusian, for whom song is the rhythmic and forceful conveying of the words—together, of course, with all the vocal devices used by the singer. Indeed, many flamencos prefer to sing *al golpe*, without guitar, using only knuckles on the table. In Jerez I can hear this almost whenever I like: I only have to come across El Monea, not himself a performing singer, though brother and cousin to famous ones. A drink (and especially the sight of a pretty woman) is enough to spark him off and, if others gather round or he likes the encouragement, we get flamenco song in its oldest, purest form.

But though the melody is secondary, it helps to know why it seems so strange to us. The strangeness of flamenco stems partly from the fact that our Western music, whether classical, folk, or pop, is almost all based on major or minor scales. If we hear a tune in, say, the key of C, we *know* the way it

Figure 8. Palmero and cantaor *a golpe* Antonio El Monea.

goes up and down the scale, and we feel it has ended when it returns to the note C, especially if it does so from G, the fifth or dominant note of the scale. In saying this I am using musical jargon, which I am trying to avoid. Many people—educated, intelligent, cultured people—happen not to have learned to read music. And there is no need to have done so in order to enjoy it, either flamenco or Mozart. Indeed, only a tiny handful of flamencos can read music, whether singers, guitarists, or "flamencologists."

For purposes of explanation it will be simpler if you consider every scale as though it were played on the white notes only of the piano (well, almost only; I go into it in a bit more detail in chapter 4 on the guitar). Starting on C and going up the keyboard playing only the white keys until you reach the next C produces the familiar major scale. (I shall refer to every tune in the major as though it started on C.) Similarly, if you start on A and go up playing only the white keys, you get the minor scale. For the Andalusian mode or scale, however, you do the same thing starting on E. This makes a flamenco song, at least until we are accustomed to it, sound to us as though it starts and stops in the middle of nowhere. The odds are that you will only have ever heard this scale if you have listened to early church music in the Phrygian mode. Familiarity. The Andalusians have been singing that way nobody knows how long, but probably at least a thousand years, so of course it seems familiar to them. You can do it in less time.

A thousand years would take us back to the days of Gregorian chant, which shares one trait with flamenco: that of singing many notes to one syllable of the words. In both languages it is called *melisma*, which is a technical term of music to us, but an everyday one to Andalusians. At first, these weavings and wanderings of the voice on one syllable may seem an extra impediment to your following an unfamiliar tune in an unfamiliar scale, and certainly to your understanding what the song is about. To the flamenco they are at least as important as the tune, which in any case is likely to be skeletal. For the deeper and more tragic the song form, the more primitive its "tune." In the case of the siguiriya or the soleá, the tune (as you and I under-stand the term) is often an ascent through the first four or five notes of the scale, followed by a descent to the starting note. The emotional effect and power of the song lies in the way the singer weaves his voice round it, in the quality of the voice itself, in the words, in the emotional force he manages to convey, and in the use of quarter tones—notes that do not exist in our music and which sound as though the singer is singing a bit flat. I shall deal with all of these, but first I want to add something on the melody.

While the deepest and most tragic song forms are woven round elemen-tary tunes, others have more recognizable—and pleasing—ones. Most *tien-tos* would take little adaptation to become music you could enjoy without having any acquaintance with flamenco. Indeed, this happens. I have heard a carol at a *zambomba,* or Christmas party, sung by two women. One was quintessentially flamenca, a Gypsy girl from the Barrio Santiago, the most exclusively Gypsy district in Andalusia; the other was a singer of non-flamenco music who was immensely popular throughout Spain. It was not flamenco, but it clearly exploited the form of the tiento.

Since the nineteenth century, a form has arisen called the *cantiña.* The most popular of its many variants is the *alegrías* (CD track 8). It is nearly all in the major key, and only at the end sometimes dips down into the Anda-lusian mode. Remember that because flamenco is based on the E mode, the music will sound as if it is in major so long as it moves chiefly around the E mode's upper notes—C, F, and G—since these are important notes in estab-lishing the key of C major. The melody of the alegrías hovers around these notes but usually returns to E instead of C at the end. Its tunes are therefore easily familiar to us. The man who was of the most help to my getting to know the song forms looked baffled when I said I did not need help with the alegrías: I was focusing on the tunes, while he was thinking of rhythms and expression, and neither of us realized we were looking in different directions. The alegrías is as rhythmically complex as any other form and should be appreciated as a dance, because its rhythms and counterrhythms are rich and complex. Indeed, for dancers it is one of the three most important forms. Nevertheless, its tune is immediately accessible to us, and the guitar harmonies—chords on C, F, and G—are those of the vamp accompaniment to folk song. Incidentally, this is one reason the major and minor scales became so universally accepted in Western music: of all the possible scales using the white piano keys, those built on C and A lend themselves most readily to harmonization. The guitar accompaniment to the alegrías has all the harmonic originality of "My Darling Clementine." That the Andalusians return to it so often, amid the rich and strange originality of their other music, gives us the clue that we should listen, not to tune, nor to harmony, but to the rhythmic subtlety inside its trotting tempo, to the expressive harshness of the voice, and—if we can—to the words.

If the tunes of the alegrías are easy, the bulería (CD track 6), which is the most popular of all forms today, has no melody of its own at all. No one can yet define it, for it is a form still in the making, but its essence is rhythmic, not melodic. In fact, the bulería can be sung to almost any tune, a point brought home to me at the birthday party of a young flamenco dancer. When he started to cut the cake, the whole troupe sang "Happy Birthday." I squirmed to hear that dreary apology of a song in those surroundings. But then someone called out, *Po' bulería thtá vé!* (Now let's do it as a bulería!), and the whole company transformed the silly tune almost beyond recognition by singing it to the bulería's complicated cross-rhythms. The effect was so electric that the cake-cutter launched himself into the dance down the length of the room, cake knife still in hand.

So, if we are not to focus on either tune or harmony, and if we leave for the moment the question of rhythm, we need to focus on those other ingredients mentioned above, in order to enjoy the pull of the song.

Perhaps the key lies in realizing that for a flamenco what comes first is expressing strong feeling and communicating it. He is not interested in sounding or looking pretty. This truth applies as much to dance and guitar as it does to song. The dancer may be graceful, but the first quality of the dance is expressive force. Likewise, the beautiful sound that John Williams can draw from a concert guitar does not interest the flamenco guitarist. The lower action of the flamenco guitar helps the *tocaor* (player) create driving rhythms and produces brighter, often harsher tones. If the sound is sometimes rough, it doesn't matter. This generalization is only partly true: guitarists such as Paco de Lucía, Manolo Sanlúcar, or, in England, Paco Peña have as much control of tone as the best classical guitarist. Likewise, many dancers lean toward the sinuous grace of Merché Esmeralda more than the Gypsy force of Manuela Carrasco. But while Paco de Lucía's recording of Joaquín Rodrigo's *Concierto de Aranjuez* is one of the best, when he is playing a traditional flamenco form, force is paramount.

And so it is with the song: forceful expression matters more than a fine singing voice. This is not to say that fine voices don't exist: Enrique Morente's baritone (and his musicianship) could have put him up in the class of Plácido Domingo or José Carreras, had he so chosen. But the more tragic song forms must have dated from the days of persecution of outcast peoples. Before 1800 all is conjecture, but the words I quote in the section on the petenera give a heart-rending glimpse of people, Jewish or Moorish, driven by the Inquisition to live outside of society, while there are other indicators that the Gypsies were hounded by the civil law. As for those Andalusians who are neither Gypsy nor Jewish nor Moorish, this is a land where the peasants have been dispossessed. Unless they were given work on the vast properties—the so-called *latifundios*—they starved. Hunger is the dominant childhood memory of friends of mine many years younger than me. It seems pretty clear that flamenco developed as the music of the outcasts and the dispossessed. It is reasonable to compare their lot with that of the black slaves of the New World. Although parallels with the blues and jazz are dangerous and the differences striking, old recordings of blues singers show how often they had hoarse voices, as well as how expressive these could be. Flamenco demands not only strong feeling, but strong communication of it to the listener. Or at least that is how it has developed: every flamenco knows the story of Silverio coping with his grief, sitting through the night by the body of his dead son, singing siguiriyas to him. But apart from such instances, flamenco needs a singer to express and listeners to react. The harsh voices that emerged from the forges and caves and fields have come to be prized, especially among the Gypsies; and the strangling of the voice in the throat has come to be one of the climactic moments of a song, a way of expressing violent emotion.

The singer conveys strong feelings with his body language as well as his voice; gesture and facial expression are part of the song. It is the norm to perform seated (except when singing for dancers), but from the waist upward every part of the body is used. When going round the singing competitions that take place every year, I found it intriguing to try to distinguish between those whose expression and gestures seemed to grow out of the pain that the song expressed, and those who assumed violent expression and gesture to help them put emotional force into their song. Either way, the clenched fists and agonized gestures help the singer to bring out and release the emotion. I am reminded of Blaise Pascal's advice—that if you don't believe in God, go down on your knees and put your hands in position to pray, and faith will come. This has been confirmed for me by a singing guru whose pupils are very successful. He says that if you adopt the physical signs of pain it helps conjure up the force of feeling.

The melismas—the weavings of the voice round a single syllable—are also a part of this search for expressive force, although they are also a musical characteristic of ancient singing that has survived in flamenco. The singer usually starts with a series of *ayes*, as though overcome with grief. This habit has even carried over from the tragic forms into the festive ones, where it can be no more than convention, and is used by the singer to check his intonation. But it is still usually more than convention: an old man passes my window most evenings, singing siguiriyas to himself; but more often than not he stays with the introductory *ayes*, dragging them up from inside himself, as though from some deep private grief. Perhaps it is a kind of ancestral memory. A manuscript of about 1740 describes a Gypsy dancer from Triana performing in great houses (just as Miguel de Cervantes's Gitanilla had done a century before). It says the song starts with "a series of sighs which they call the galley-slave's groan [*queja de galera*]."

In the course of the song, according to the singer's mood or instinct, the melismas will return as a way of stressing key moments. And in the case of the *fandangos* and their various offshoots, the song will end with the voice weaving and tumbling in melismas to the final note. They are not formless or ad lib; in fact, their length and shape are very much a part of the art. A melisma that is too short strikes the ear as perfunctory, but if it is too long the shape is lost and the power of the song dissipated—art gives way to showmanship. This is one reason why in eastern Andalusia, where the mining song called the *taranta* comes from, they reckon only a very good singer can perform it well. It is a song of such tragic intensity that its final cadences are hard to get right. Most singers take refuge in less intense versions of it, such as the *minera* or the more florid *cartagenera*. And in western Andalusia, where the taranta is not indigenous, I have never heard it well sung. I illustrate the art of melisma in chapter 5 with two recordings of the *granaína* (CD tracks 14 and 15).

And what of quarter tones? Since they exist in Arabic music, I imagine they come from that source, or through it from Persian or Indian origins. In my experience of flamenco, quarter tones always involve a flattening of the tone, never a sharpening. You are most likely to hear them if you are in Andalusia for Holy Week, for they are a feature of the *saeta* sung to the processional tableaux in the street (CD track 21). Elsewhere they often come at the top of the curve of a phrase, though some singers sustain them: I have heard Antonio Nuñez "El Chocolate" sing a *carcelera* (prison song) in which he held a long note flattened by a quarter tone, with extraordinary effect. Curiously, it did not sound flat so much as rich; and his guitarist, Antonio Jero, had the instinct to hold his playing, leaving the sung note on its own. I find that the effect of the flattened quarter tone is usually to add a touch of gray, desolate pathos. In classical music, the only thing that I can think of like this effect comes in certain gray moments of Schubert's last quintet. But then, El Chocolate is a great singer, at his best in the tragic song forms.

An expressive singer needs listeners to react. It helps the performers to have an audience that is audibly alive, rather than the hushed respect of our tradition. It can go both ways: the late Manuel el Sordera, faced with the racket being made by one audience, was reduced to pleading with the crowd to enable him to hear his guitarist (*sordera* means deafness, although he wasn't). But any good performer is buoyed by the *jaleo*, the encouragement expressed in such interjections from the audience as *azá! qué sabe! toma que te toma! vamo' pa' allá!* or just the name of the singer or (for a woman) *guapa!* (pretty), let alone by the explosion of approval that greets the end of a verse or a *desplante* (climactic point) in the dance. When away on tour they just have to be professional and do without. Thus when Cumbre Flamenca and, more recently, Corazón Flamenco came to London, they ran straight through the places where at home they would wait for applause, and they started with upbeat, even non-flamenco items and sang them through in order to warm the audience up. It is not that the audience is unappreciative or cold, just that it goes against all our habits to make any noise during a performance; and respect for the artist adds to our inhibition. This is changing. In May 2000 José Mercé sang in London in the most un-flamenco of venues, the Barbican Hall, and was so put at ease by the audience's warmth that he began to sing *a gusto*. The result was possibly the best flamenco singing London has ever heard.

Strong feeling successfully conveyed to listeners who react: this is encapsulated by the flamenco's term of praise for good singing: *me dice*.

39

Figure 9. José Mercé, singer. Photo: Amparo Ruiz. Courtesy of *El Olivo*
Magazine

The Song

The singer's rhythmic subtlety does not, I think, make the song harder for us, though it makes it impossible to write palos such as the seguiriya on the music stave: the composer Maurice Ohana, working with the singer Antonio Mairena, was only able to suggest tentatively that it is sung in something like 7/8 time, as against the different time scheme of guitarist and dancer. But just as quarter tones enable a singer to curve over one phrase or fall away from another, he uses a rhythmic fluidity that cannot be notated to curve and mold his song. Thus, the singer's note seldom falls exactly with the beat on the bar. He will either anticipate it slightly or delay it, so that the song sounds as though it is only very loosely attached to any set form. And yet, in fact, the opposite is true: the singer's rhythmic discipline is such that if you keep strict count (or if you put a metronome to his performance) you will find that, without being *on* the beat, he stays precisely *with* it throughout his song. This may be said of jazz players, too. But in their case the beat itself is always audible and heavily marked. The flamenco singer has to carry it inside him. Hence the accolade "he has good compás." To sing with this much rhythmic flexibility and yet give the dancer a reliable framework on which to weave her own rhythms suggests that the phrase means a lot more than merely "he can keep in time."

The words are crucial in any kind of song. In this respect those of us who are not Andalusian are handicapped. It is usually not even enough to know Spanish—not even to *be* Spanish. One difficulty is that Andalusian speech softens consonants often to the point of inaudibility. Gypsy speech takes this characteristic still further; many of them find it impossible to get their tongues round any form of *s*. Enrique el Canastero, who maintains the Sacromonte cave of his famous mother, María la Canastera, asked me to help him learn some English phrases. We were sitting on the wall outside enjoying the autumn sun while, to my private amusement, he worked on a stick with his knife ("Can you chin the cosh [cut a stick]?" was almost a password among English Gypsies at one time). What would he like to learn?

"The cassette costs a thousand pesetas." When I told him, he threw up his hands: "Oh! Those English *s*'s!" This sounded better than it reads, for it came out as "The cahé coh a thouha pehehah" and "Ay! ehoh eheh ingleheh!" End of English lessons. To this difficulty you must add that, by a convention of the song, the singer distorts the vowel on any held note so that it becomes something like *eouuu*. Even if you understand Spanish, the only way you are likely to be able to appreciate how the singer conveys the meaning is by living in the south of Spain and acclimatizing, as you do to the heat of the sun. There is no linguistic suntan cream to help the process.

There is also a sprinkling of words that are not Spanish at all: either they are in the Gypsy Caló (which is an offshoot of one of the languages of India), or else they are derived from old prison slang. If you do speak Spanish— and can follow the Andalusian accent—it is not quite so bad as I make it sound, for you can soon pick up the few dozen Gypsy words that commonly occur. I list most of them in an appendix. Even so, when I can't follow the words of a song, I find it more profitable to ask help from a Gypsy than a gachó. For this reason I have included words to songs in chapter 5 on the palos in the hopes of giving a taste of the song's mood.

3

The Dance

Ballet is up; flamenco is down.

La Presi

It is with the dance as with the song and the guitar: the art of flamenco is on the move, influenced by the fashions of the day, the demands of the market, and the individuals whose success influences others—some through their mastery, others through their originality—or their showmanship. Every time I need to make a general statement, the exceptions and the variations leap to mind. Yet, without the general comment and the mainstream trend, we will never get anywhere. So in all that follows it must be borne in mind that I am characterizing or describing *most* flamenco dancing, *as it is today*.

I have already said that, however ancient the dance may be, the song governs it. But in chapter 2 I also said that, for the flamenco, song is first and foremost rhythm and rhythm is in itself potential dance. The rhythm comes mainly from the guitar, from clapping (*palmas*), finger snapping (*pitos*), or tapping with knuckles or stick, as well, of course, as from the song and from the dancer's own feet. The guitar gives the meter (compás); the dancer's feet generate the rhythm and shape of the dance; and the clapping reinforces the measure and beats variations within it. All these are a part of the art. There is a big difference, for instance, between the soft clapping of the *palma sorda*

Figure 10. Dancers three: Antonio El Pipa with Irene Carrasco and Manuela Nuñez. Photo: Miguel Angel González. Courtesy of the Centro Andaluz de Flamenco

and the rifle-crack accuracy of the *palma alta.* What is more, a slight varia-tion in the loudness or sharpness of a single clap throws the rhythm askew: clapping is also an art. And then again, the patterns can be so tricky—in the case of the bulerías, for instance—that you don't join in unless you really know it. "That's something the tourists like to do," a tablao dancer told me.

Figure 11. The intensity of the dance: María del Mar Moreno with the singer Juana la del Pipa. Photo: Miguel Angel González. Courtesy of the Centro Andaluz de Flamenco

"They clap their hands, and if they're on vacation having a good time, we're not going to insult people by shutting them up. But it's terrible for the artist—it throws us."

I made no mention of castanets (*palillos*). Nowadays, if you see them used, you have to doubt the authenticity of the dancer. Listen to Pílar López, a great dancer now retired: "Palillos were introduced by *bailarines* (ballet dancers) doing flamenco—like the shawl and the train dress." In other words, they were introduced when flamenco became a stage spectacle in the latter part of the nineteenth century. And that is how they are still used: either in the flamencoized forms of ballet such as boleros, or else in shows put on for foreign audiences—which is why so many foreigners associate them with flamenco.

Or listen to the late Regla Ortega: "They were never used in real flamenco. For *tanguillos, Huelva fandangos, sevillanas,* yes; but real flamenco, no." The *Huelva fandangos* and the *sevillanas* are folk dances that show flamenco influence. That she included *tanguillos,* a festive dance from Cádiz, I find interesting, for castanets appeared there long before flamenco. Cádiz was noted for its dancers as early as Roman times, when they used the *crotalum,* a form of castanet. This is not to deny the skill needed to play them, nor their rhythmic richness—in the right place, which is not flamenco. Today, even in the sevillanas, castanets seem to me to cripple the dance by making impossible the dancer's graceful twirling of fingers and wrist.

Flamenco is essentially a solo art, but today increasingly you see dancing in pairs or small groups, as well as the sort of flamenco ballet done so well in Carlos Saura's film versions of Federico García Lorca and Manuel de Falla. However, the solo dance, with the singer *pa' atrás* (standing behind and singing for the dancer), done to the accompaniment of guitar and palmas—this is still the pure thing, and the best to watch.

Also solo, but with a difference that is perhaps one of generation, is dancing with a fan, in the train-dress (*bata de cola*), or with a shawl (*mantón*). Whichever the song form, these dances always tend toward balletic grace rather than flamenco force and so seem to belong more to a previous generation. In a sense, this is strictly true. They were developed in the late nineteenth century, when flamenco became a fashionable performance in the *cafés cantantes.* There is a touch of Edwardian elegance to them, and they are

Figure 12. Singing standing (*pa' atrás*) for a dancer. The classic trio of authentic flamenco: singer, guitarist, palmero. Ana de los Reyes, Jesús Algarrado "El Guardia," and José Rubichi.

mostly still performed by such grandes dames as Merché Esmeralda and Matilde Coral (both of whom you may have seen in Saura's documentary film *Sevillanas*) or by Japanese dancers, who seem to feel more affinity with graceful than with forceful movement. The *baile del mantón* or shawl dance belongs to the same category but is still often performed, famously by Blanca del Rey in Madrid and even by younger flamencos.

This contrasting of grace with force is linked in many people's minds to other oppositions that can arouse strong opinions. Gypsy dancers often claim to have learned everything from their family, and as the Gypsy style tends to concentrate more on forceful rhythms, they sometimes affect to decry those dancers who have trained in dance academies, where graceful movement tends also to be given importance. And so you will find the tendency to oppose force/Gypsy/family-trained to grace/non-Gypsy/academy-trained. If I had to choose between them, it would be for force/family/Gypsy. But luckily I don't have to choose, because, like so many arguments, the debate distorts things by overstating the contrast. The dancer's talent is more important than the blend in the style. Furthermore, the claim of having been family trained, often made by Gypsies, is a myth. With rare exceptions, today's dancers are professional performers with a technique that couldn't be picked up in the family. The fabulous Carmen Amaya was an exception to every rule. What *can* be said is that the rich counterrhythms of an Angelita Vargas, who is a forceful dancer rather than a graceful one, are rewarding to watch, whereas I have yet to see a dancer who could compel my attention by grace alone, without force. Grace is a quality of dance the world over. Force is a flamenco quality.

As for dancing in pairs or small groups, if you listen to the purists, you will think nothing can be pure flamenco that is not danced solo. Yet flamencos, both Gypsy and gachó, perform in pairs and groups, not only for the tourist, but for their own kind too. Indeed my irritation at being shut out of one such performance for which I had not thought necessary to book was diverted only when I saw the fury of an eminent and senior Gypsy flamenco who had made the same mistake. But in such groups, the dancers coordinate their movements and rhythms without exactly repeating one another. Figure 13 shows a rehearsal for a performance. Three of the six dancers happen to be facing one way and three the other. In the performance they may well do it differently. And while the rhythms rapped out by the feet of the women are here synchronic, the man's feet are marking a counterrhythm.

It is commonly thought that flamenco dance is improvised. So it is, but in certain restricted ways. In a review in the London *Times,* the dance correspondent panned a fine performance under the delusion that it was not improvised and so could not be "pure" flamenco. One wonders how she imagined you can perform on the professional stage, with a professional lighting design, without coordination among the performers—even in a solo dance. In that instance the dancer was Charo Espino, and she danced one of the finest soleares I have seen, illustrated on the cover. What might have been improvised in a club could not possibly be unchoreographed in the professional theater, at least insofar as the timing of movements across the stage is concerned. But when I went back to see her again, her soleares were different. The movement over the stage and the synchronization with the singers and guitarists were indeed the same, but the dancer's mood was different, so the dance was, too: Charo Espino is a genuine flamenco. A group of dancers, each doing his or her own thing on stage, would be more like fairground bumper cars. Yet for a performance to be long enough to make it worth the public's while to pay their money and come to the show, you must have variety. The variety includes dancing in groups, whether for an international tour or for a performance to aficionados in their hometown. The world has changed, and flamenco has moved on since Gustave Doré's pictures from the 1870s of barefoot Gypsy girls dancing for pennies in the tavern.

Above all, today the flamenco needs to earn a living. A singer or guitarist may get recording contracts; the dancer must be seen. Live perform-

Figure 13. Asymmetry and improvisation. Three dancers in this rehearsal are facing one way; three, the other. In performance they may do it differently. Note also that the movements of the women are synchronized, while the man's are in counterrhythm. All these dancers are now launched on their careers.

ance means in effect the peñas, the tablaos, and the theater. The peñas, with their involved and knowledgeable audiences, offer the purer—and more improvised—flamenco. But they wouldn't of themselves keep the performers in bread and butter. The tablaos and the theaters both make their commercial demands and condition the art. But both help the flamenco dancer earn a living.

Nevertheless, flamenco remains in essence an improvised art in that it depends for its quality on the performer's mood and form at the moment of performance. Blanca del Rey danced recently in a large theater that was poorly attended (for reasons not connected with her artistry). During a tiento-tango she moved downstage and incorporated into her dance a counting of heads, followed by an audible *po' lo meno' diez* (at least ten). There were in fact some two hundred, but they cheered her.

While the dancer usually expresses the mood of the song, the dance is abstract in that the movements do not represent anything. So it might seem as if flamenco ballet is a contradiction in terms, for ballet—at least traditional ballet—does have a meaning and does tell a story, even when done in flamenco style. In recent years, thanks to Carlos Saura's films, the most widely known performers have been Antonio Gades and Cristina Hoyos, who have classical as well as flamenco training. Gades started as a classical dancer and learned flamenco, and Cristina Hoyos started as a flamenco *bailaora*. They met in the middle. Gades's staged *Carmen* in 1996 was a strange mixture of Bizet, flamenco, and Latin American music, yet the blend was successful and told the story with powerful intensity. So perhaps here, as elsewhere, the quality of performance is more important than theory or principles. Gades's work can be put beside the many other attempts to find a way forward for an art that, to be worthwhile, cannot remain what it has been in the past. And the fact is that there are, and have been since Carmen Amaya, great flamenco dancers who have performed in storytelling ballets and films: Mario Maya, Manolete, Manuela Vargas, and Carmen Cortés, to name only a few (and only Gypsy ones at that). The Spanish language marks the difference: the classically trained dancer (whether or not also dancing flamenco) is a *bailarín*; the flamenco dancer is a *bailaor* or *bailaora*. Prejudices run deep on the subject, and you will hear flamencos, especially in western Andalusia, say that Mario Maya is a bailarín—the word pronounced with scorn as though he were also somehow a traitor to his kind. Yet in pure

Figures 14 and 15. Engravings by Gustave Doré, 1874.

flamenco, there is no male dancer that I would rather see, except for his cousin Manolete. It needs to be remembered that these two come from Granada in eastern Andalusia, and in Spain allegiance to one's own town or province tends to be fiercely chauvinist.

Four of the general characteristics of the dance have already cropped up: it is individual, forceful, downward, and introvert. It is also abstract and ecstatic. The last four terms can do with a bit of expansion.

Downward. At the start of this chapter I quoted La Presi, an experienced dancer and teacher in Granada. It was her answer to what would have been an idiotic question had I not been aware of her laconic acuteness or known she had had early ballet training while she was still a Cherokee girl in Austin, Texas, before being brought to Spain by the great flamenco dancer and teacher Ciro. It is much more than the elementary truism it might seem to be: it is a yardstick not to be discarded, for it underlies and reinforces almost everything else.

It is worth pointing out how important a part of the dance the *zapateado* is (the creation of rhythms by drumming on the ground with the feet). The dance uses the whole body, but it is largely generated by these drummed rhythms. To create its patterns, the dancer makes variations in the quality and intensity of sound by using the heel, the whole foot, the sole, and the point of the toe, as well as by scraping the sole in a brush-drum effect. All these movements tend toward a stamping downward. By the same token, there are no leaps, no upward movements of any sort. This may well date from the early Muslim prohibition of showing the leg—never forget that Andalusia was under Islamic law for the better part of eight hundred years. Only very seldom in the bulerías and *farrucas* will you even see the knee lifted, in a long pace. The downwardness of the dance also shows in the eyes, which are usually directed downward even when the face turns up.

Introvert. Listen to some dancers talking about what they do: "It goes to the solar plexus, to the center of the universe"; "You have to dance for your-

Figure 16. Cristina Hoyos, dancer. Photo: Miguel Angel González.
Courtesy of the Centro Andaluz de Flamenco

self"; "I love dancing the soleá so much that I lose myself and don't know who I am"; "It is the expression *inside you* of your happiness or sorrow." Any dance that is essentially solo is also introverted, since the dancer is not relating to anyone else. The downward direction of the eyes reinforces this, shutting the dancer inside herself. There is a current fashion (followed only by a few so far) for stopping in the dance to catch the audience's eye, as though to say, "Now wasn't that clever of me?" Except in the bulería, which is a festive, even cheeky dance, I find it a distracting gimmick and hope the fad will die.

Abstract. If flamenco is abstract, what *does* it express? "The mood of the song" is a short answer, but not an adequate one. Most (but not all) of the best dancers dance to the words of the song, so such basic emotions as happy and unhappy love, grief, anguish, anger, and so forth may be involved. But if the dancer has good technical command, the dance in large measure expresses both more and less than that. It expresses the personality of the dancer, or at least a personal reaction to the words. And there is a pervasive element of arrogant self-assertion that seems almost necessary if the personality of the dancer is to come across. Above all else, the dancer must feel confident. Antonio El Pipa, when I first saw him, was already successful (he won the Córdoba dance competition), but his reputation had yet to hit the heights. Of him, an older flamenco said to me: "Antonio is good, and I think he will be very good—when he starts to believe in his talent as much as we do." At the time, his dance expressed above all what an amiable man he was. Two years later the transformation had happened. His dancing had all the arrogant-looking command in the world. I put this beside what a German dance student told me: that she *knew* that, to look any good (and therefore to be any good) she had to appear marvelous (and therefore try to feel so). But it was hard to do so when she knew she wasn't. It was clear that, in saying this, she was thinking of her lack of technique, rather than of her person or her artistic potential. Confident command of technique would enable her to project mood and personality, which would make her technique look better—a vicious circle that I imagine is familiar to every apprentice performance artist, whatever the art, and one that only hard, persistent work would enable her to break. Though it is also true that a certain prickly pride is notable in the Gypsies—it is indeed part of our stereotypical image of Spaniards. The dancer needs to project this, which may be one reason so few outsiders ever become really good at flamenco. I used to feel that the dancer needed a measure of arrogant self-confidence. But two anecdotes suggest this is mistaken. One concerns the great Manuela Carrasco. Eva Yerbabuena, a star as yet only thirty years old, was taken when she was eleven to see her dance. "We were with her in the dressing room, and she was very shy, like me. When I saw her on stage, in make-up and dancing, she was like a child dressed up for a carnival, with another personality that enabled her to communicate with us. That hooked me." There is a dancer called Carmen Herrera (figure 17) whose quality and promise so convince me she is due for fame that I have taken many photos of her. On returning to England, I showed the pictures to friends and asked them, "How old is she?" The answers ranged from twenty-five upward. In fact, she was barely fourteen. Offstage she is a shy, polite child. Perhaps this quality has less to do with any arrogance than with the fact that performers love to perform. Andalusians seem all to love having their photo taken; when I see a good face, even on an unknown passer-by, I know I'm welcome to photograph them.

In male dancers, this self-confidence or self-assertion comes across as rampant machismo. That presents problems today, when most professional dancers are the product of dance academies, which attract relatively few raging bulls. Some of them simulate this peacock virility; in others it is replaced by display of technique; a few don't even try. I can also think of three or four leading dancers of the younger generation (such as Joaquin Grilo, Israel Galván, and Juan Antonio Tejero) for whom this is not a problem: they are certainly macho, but they are leading the dance away from the traditional projection of machismo.

But whatever the variations, the essential characteristic that emerges from the abstract nature of the dance is that the dancer expresses only himself or herself. Except in the flamenco ballets, which are currently on the increase, the dancers have none of the actor's need to get inside another's skin. The exception, however, is notable. The Gypsy dancer Carmen Cortés

Figure 17. Carmen Herrera hooks the audience at a party in 1999.
A potential star, yet offstage she was here a shy child of barely fourteen.

succeeds in recreating García Lorca's *Yerma* in a powerfully moving way without losing any of the purely flamenco expression of the bailaora.

Ecstatic. The word *duende* is bandied about by writers and broadcasters more than it is by flamencos themselves, who more usually refer to *angel* if the performer seems in inspiring form. *Duende* suggests possession. The word *ecstatic* is pretty strong stuff, too. So it needs the qualification that it refers to a tendency only. Nevertheless, the dance *is* self-involving, and the dancer can lose herself in it, as anyone who has seen Manuela Carrasco will realize. The paradox raised by her dancing concerns the extraordinary control that also characterizes her performance, and should remind us that these people are professionals, doing a professional job. This ecstatic nature of the dance arises, so it has been claimed, from its force and its intensity in continuous movement within the hypnotic repetition of the compás. It applies not only as a general description, but in one particular part of certain dances, notably the soleá. To see this requires that we go into the vexed question of those who construct a whole dance as against those whose dance consists of a series of bits added one on another. For the moment, let's leave it at that, and just go on as if all dancers had the art to shape a whole dance into a unity, as only the best ones do. In them, the dance seems understated at first, then slowly, gradually, it rises in intensity until it reaches a climax. It is at this point that you may see the torso twist and shudder, the head jerk violently from side to side, the hair fly, and the head be thrown back. Not only in the soleá: I have seen Sara Baras (before she decided to go consciously "modern") dance an alegrías that worked up to a climax that brought the audience to its feet.

I think there are some points to make about this. The first is the phenomenon of *descarga*, which means a discharge, as of electricity. The build-up of tension in the dancer (and in the singer, too) demands such release. This happens in the zapateado and in the moments of climax known as *desplantes*, which I discuss below, when the dancer does address the audience and seems to be demanding applause. A second point is that anthropologists describe primitive dance in terms similar to those I have used. They also affirm that many of the qualities of flamenco song are those of primitive song—especially of these same soleares and seguiriyas—citing the rise and fall of the melody by steps over a limited scale and the predominance of ternary rhythm. Yet another point is that many dancers (all too many!) have the technique and the rhythm but lack either the artistry, or the understanding, or perhaps just the maturity to shape a whole dance. If the shape of the dance is not there, I am tempted to doubt the ecstatic elements. I cannot convey this better than by lifting a passage from my own notes, written after watching one of the first dancers I saw. My mentor, La Presi, had given me a list of points to watch for and suggested that so long as I remembered them I should follow my own instincts—at least until I knew better:

> She used the *zapateado* less for the rhythm of the dance than to cruise back to her starting point. From there she drifted across the stage, mainly in slow grace that suddenly erupted into violent body movement on the spot, with lightning turns this way and that, her head whirling left, right, left, as though possessed. . . . Her loss of headgear at such climactic moments, first a taffeta rose, then something green, then a comb, looked to me like professional trickery. It said: "See how I have the *duende*!" and "See how my hair is disheveled! I have given you my all in this dance!" The fact that the projectile flew—one at each climax—sideways or back, never into the eye of a spectator, just may have been luck. Perhaps. But I don't like being hoodwinked—especially by one whose skill and art make it unnecessary. I kept hoping someone would get a comb in the eye.

Later I did know better. I had seen great dancers such as Juana Amaya and recognized to what extent this young dancer had been imitating her. Juana Amaya's particular trait is her sudden eruption into violent movement out of simmering stillness. But the dancer I describe above was imitating

Figure 18. Juana Amaya, dancer. Photo: Amparo Ruiz. Courtesy of *El Olivo* Magazine

the mannerisms without seeing that Juana Amaya's dance is all of a unity and grows slowly, slowly in its intensity until it reaches those ecstatic moments.

The points La Presi gave me to help me distinguish good from bad were few and simple: "Always look at a dancer's hands: the hands have to be smooth; if there's any kind of brusque movement, it has to be some demand of the rhythm. Look for a good clean line. And look for a shape in the dance. If it has those three elements, and you've liked what you've seen, you can feel pretty comfortable that you've seen something of quality." She was referring only to the woman's dance, where the arms, hands, and fingers move in a continuous flow, seemingly independent of her other movements. Most dancers manage the arms well; only the better ones give the good clean line that conveys a hardness, a steel-spring tension of the body. And few can shape a whole dance.

The man's dance does not have the ornamental wrist and finger movements of the woman's. His fingers are held together, straight or cupped, and the twirling at the wrist is usually done as an inward motion rather than both in and out. Apart from this and a more rigid stance, the other differences stem mainly from his disadvantage, for the woman can do a lot not only with the constant movement of her arms and hands, but with her swirling skirt as well. The man has only a jacket, waistcoat, or kerchief to manipulate. He can hold it and turn it back, or he can take it off and swing it over his shoulder. It's not much, compared to the woman's dress. In the old days, men had a virtual monopoly on the zapateado. Gypsy women used to dance barefoot, though a nineteenth-century writer tells of the fandango being danced by women with much zapateado. Today, not even that is the man's preserve. Since the great Carmen Amaya started incorporating zapateado into her dance in the 1920s, it has begun to take over the dance for both men and women. Incidentally, when Carmen Amaya was young, her father put her in trousers. In later life, she commented that "trousers are unforgiving; they show up every mistake and they give you nothing to take hold of." We outsiders may not always appreciate the rhythmic subtleties of the zapateado, since we do not have the underlying compás deep in our bones; and I for one do not usually get enthusiastic about those dancers (usually men, and there are many of them) whose dance is zapateado to the virtual exclusion of all other types of movement. However, on the occasions when it does grip, I know the dancer is unusually good. Of the established male dancers, Juan Ramírez can both build a whole dance out of it and keep me riveted, as can José Fernández and Gabriel Muñoz. Others, such as Javier Barón, Diego Llori, Israel Galván, Joaquín Grilo, and Juan Antonio Tejero, always make a complete dance with the zapateado woven into it.

This creeping growth of the zapateado has been blamed on the dance academies. The fact is that the dance grows out of the rhythms it generates, and these rhythms are endlessly subtle, so the zapateado tends to occupy most of the practice time.

The use of clothing as an adjunct—while I am airing personal prejudices—can cut both ways. A talent for dancing is not necessarily accompanied by good taste or color sense. Both the dancers' dresses and the so-called flamenco dresses that Andalusian women wear at festivals are always colorful, and sometimes hideously so. (The dresses are by no means the same: the frills and froth of the so-called flamenco dresses—also called *faralaes* [frills]—make them too heavy to dance in.) Appearance on television tends to bring out any such color-blindness in the dancer, sometimes memorably. One lass appeared on Seville television holding what looked like a fat bunch of entrails dangling from green Spanish moss. Then she let it drop, and one realized that it was a *bata de cola* (a dress with a train). The dress was green, and the train, feet deep in slaughterhouse frills. For all I know she may have danced well, but the dress compelled my morbid attention rather as a road accident might.

La Presi's description of the hands and arms is a guide rather than a universal rule (there *are* no rigid rules). Among the finest women dancers I have

63

seen—Manuela Carrasco, Carmen Cortés, Blanca del Rey, Eva Yerbabuena, and Juana Amaya—Juana's use of her hands is all her own. I quoted earlier from my notes on one of her imitators. Here are some taken on a soleá I saw Juana Amaya herself dance:

> She is as idiosyncratic as she is powerful. She does not keep the hands and fingers moving: there are sudden movements, movements of one hand only, clenched fists—and the continuous and graceful twirling of wrist and fingers is only one among these many hand uses. Her habit, at least early in the dance, is to alternate zapateado with standing still—if you can use the word "still" for such simmering intensity. But the dance is long; a symphony, not a gavotte. Gradually she begins to move into *punteado*: much *paseo* at first and only then *mudanzas*. She seems to build up the whole (i.e. give it perceptible *form*) by slightly shortening each section, while increasing its intensity. And you *feel* the form, you sense that we haven't got there yet. When she does "get there" it is a climax long expected—and not cheapened by tricks of hair decoration or whatever. The *convulsiones* and *torsiones* are there, but they have grown out of all that has gone before, and they don't seem like professional performers' tricks. Whether they are or not, doesn't worry me: she is an artist; a dancer of caliber; and the fact that it may be all choreographed is her business—it *feels* as though it is spontaneously emerging from the song. This is some of the best dancing I have seen. It engrosses—and drains you.

The characteristic that La Presi called "a good clean line," which I tried to characterize as the supple tautness of a steel spring, goes much further than that. The best dancers achieve an economy of movement that makes the expressive force of their dance the greater for being contained. This quality of contained force is called *asentamiento*, which implies a settling in. La Presi told me, "There's no magic word, no technique for getting it: it's a final understanding of flamenco. It is the most difficult thing to describe. It goes to the center of the universe, and it goes to the solar plexus. It takes a long time to reach this feeling. People are conditioned to seeing twenty-year-olds on stage, but with flamenco you have to get a little bit of age on, and that's when you start seeing something good."

By the same token, when the elderly dance it is always worth watching. El Farruco, who died recently, much mourned, was a self-taught Gypsy from Seville who danced for many decades. If you have seen Carlos Saura's film *Flamenco* you will remember him dancing with his grandson. It is so economical: a twitch of the hip . . . a step . . . a flick of the wrist . . . a slight turn of the head . . . hardly anything, but it makes compulsive watching. The reason lies, partly at least, in the placement of these small moves. They are accents in the rhythm of the dance and do not necessarily fall on the beat of the basic measure. So they convey all the unseen, unheard elements of that rhythm.

My meaning here may be obscure, so I will try two comparisons. In a symphonic movement in 4/4 time, the music will seldom if ever plonk out the 1–2–3–4 of the time signature. But we are so used to that underlying regular beat that it remains present inside us, and what we actually hear takes its rhythmic life by varying on it, by pulling or pushing against it. The ingredients of music are difficult to express in words—somebody once said that talking about music is like dancing about architecture—so perhaps it may be easier to compare it with the rhythms of words in verse. Shakespeare's lines are based on iambic pentameter, which goes

$$\cup - \cup - \cup - \cup - \cup -$$

as in the line (mine, not Shakespeare's)

> The dáy she wént to tówn and bóught a hát.

But this regular measure, which surfaces so ploddingly in my line, *underlies* the verse, so that

> Oh, that this too, too solid flesh should melt

comes as a rich variation on it. We hear it as such in our mind's ear, pushing and pulling against the underlying regular measure. In the case of flamenco, it is not too hard to learn those underlying measures (I give them in chapter 5), but they are not ingrained in us, in the way that every flamenco has had them ingrained in him from the cradle.

Nevertheless, in old people's dance, the accents that their movements give to the measure are so sparse, so economical that we *can* feel and see the way they push and pull against at rhythm. In fact, one of the most memorable pieces of dancing I have seen involved Enrique el Cojo, in extreme old age, at a ceremony given to honor him. Lame since childhood and now almost incapacitated, he had been brought onstage, painfully and slowly and supported on either side as he managed first one foot then another, for the speeches at the start of the program. He was helped again later in the program for the dance, this time on Matilde Coral's arm with two other dancers assisting. The guitars played bulerías, and the three women danced in turn before him. And then he began to move. A slight twist of the wrist, a tentative shuffle, a twitch at his jacket—his face started to come alive, his feet began to work. And he danced. And as he danced he began to move over the floor. Nobody was hovering over him now. And this was not all. When he had finished, the guitars started to play siguiriyas. And that old, old man, this time without any starting help, danced a whole siguiriya, his face absorbed, lost deep in the dance, but intensely alive. It was the stuff of miracles, but it happened.

From the old to the very young. I said a moment ago that the underlying rhythms, such as I give in chapter 5, are ingrained in every flamenco from the cradle. He has been hearing them literally all his life. This is probably the main reason so few foreigners ever become really good. Dance students tell me that the bulería is the hardest to learn. Yet the six-year-old Lorena (figure 19) has been doing it with style for more than a year. Another possible reason for the Andalusian's superiority in dancing flamenco was suggested to me

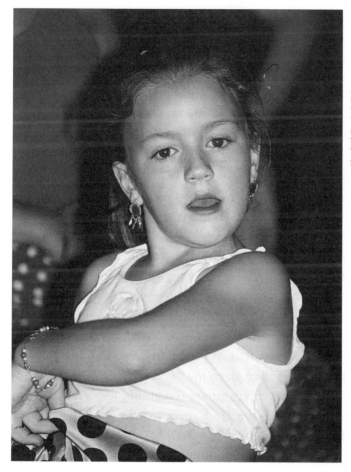

Figure 19. Starting young. Every line in Lorena's body shows the true dancer, and her absorption in the dance is patent.

by a young American who exclaimed in exasperation, "How the heck can I ever hope to dance like them, when they're so darned graceful, just walking down the street?" My own reaction to this was to think of Isabel, my green-grocer, a comfortably built fifty-year-old, who keeps me abreast of the news of the Gypsy quarter. An emphatic "no" is accompanied by a flinging up of her hand, and she ends the gesture with a flick of the wrist as graceful and expressive as any dancer's movement.

The third element that it helps to watch for is the construction and shaping of the whole dance. Theoretically, this lies in the combining of certain ingredients. But in practice, in every good dance that I have seen, the shape was what the dancer made you feel it to be: it never depended on any theoretical form. It varies both with the palo and with the dancer. The palos tend to influence the construction of the dance by their different characteristics: the tiento, for example is more stately and tends to demand the more graceful *punteado* (steps), while the alegrías, with its steady trotting tempo, tends to invite the rhythmic variations and the counterrhythms of the zapateado.

As for the individual dancer, some tend more toward punteado—themselves consisting of the *paseo* (walking movement) and the more intricate *mudanzas* (literally, variations). Others use the punteado as little more than a break in the zapateado. All these are ingredients that go into the shaping of a dance. But in whatever proportion they may be put together, each section draws to a close in a sort of climax that is called a *desplante*. Don't ask me for a clear definition: five dancers have given me five almost incompatibly differing descriptions. All they have in common is that they feel it to be a great bit of the dance, and that it brings the dance either to a climax or to a cadence or pausing point. The ending of the dance, called a *remate*, varies with the dance form. But in many cases, both in song and dance, it involves a change to a fast tempo.

It may be worth adding a short postscript on the desplante. In Andalusia, where audiences react audibly, every desplante brings applause. When abroad, faced with audiences who are accustomed to maintaining silence to the end, they tend to play it down, poor dears. But not always. A troupe of competent performers who toured Britain recently so played up their desplantes that they forced the audience to applaud, and having done so, added more of them to make sure the audience had got the message. It was a successful ploy, and deserved to be.

In 1995 the Irish dancing of *Riverdance* took a huge audience by storm. When the show was expanded, it incorporated American tap dance and flamenco, the other two western forms of dance that generate rhythms with the feet. Many people, like me, found the flamenco section disappointing. This was not because of the performers. María Pagés is a good dancer, and her guitarist, Rafael Riqueni, is a brilliant player. The fact is, the music was not flamenco. It was composed by Bill Whelan and had the insistent beat of the Irish dance, which, while it, too, uses broken rhythms, does not build on an Andalusian compás. The dancing of María Pagés with body, arms, and hands was good, if as idiosyncratic as she always is. But insofar as she used the techniques of the zapateado, she did so to conform to the beat of the band, not to weave counterrhythms round it. I don't see how she could have done a flamenco zapateado since she did not have a flamenco compás to build her rhythms on. One of the striking features of the show was that, whether with hard- or soft-shoe, the Irish dancers, in keeping with that style's tradition, use feet and legs only: the body and arms are held immobile. It is as though they, too, were under some Koranic prohibition, though of arm rather than leg. But flamenco dance uses all parts of the body. You could say that both Irish and tap are dances *of* the feet, while flamenco is dance *generated by* the feet. The body conveys the sensual vitality, the head becomes a major source of expression in the violent movements of the climactic moments, and the arms work constantly as ornamentation.

I started by stressing that flamenco is on the move. What I have tried to do in this chapter is give some sort of a guide through a main line. It is worth emphasizing again that all orthodoxies, theories, and prescriptions can be a hindrance to enjoyment: the dance is what the dancer makes it, and it is good or bad according to how well it is done. That is the only worthwhile criterion. Personally, I regret most attempts at marrying it with modern dance, or "fusion" with jazz, rock or whatever. But that is a personal opinion and as such has no objective value. And even in that, I am inconsistent, for there is one form of innovative fusion that I enjoy: the rap bulerías of Tomasito. I first came across it at the Jerez Feria del Caballo—a week-long day-and-night festivity that only the Andalusians are hardy enough to survive. I happened to be strolling past a pavilion when a bunch of twelve-year-olds came tumbling out of it into the dusty avenue and started dancing bulerías with electric energy and in an unusual, staccato style. Their singing sounded like rap: the words nonstop, seemingly their own, interspersed with meaningless syllables, which are common in flamenco but here sounded more like rap. People began to gather round them, many of them old folk whom one might have expected to disapprove of such innovation. But they began to clap the rhythm and egg them on with jaleo. Clearly they enjoyed it, and clearly no one thought this was not the real thing. Later I realized that the dancers must have got the idea from Tomasito, who dances like a speeded-up cartoon while singing rap. His performance goes down well, both in Andalusia and (so he told me, as though it were a bigger thing) in California too; but the endorsement of the older and more traditional locals (and, indeed, of Paco Peña, who took him on tour to the United States) seems to me the truer accolade.

And so it should be. Quality of performance is what matters; theory is for theorists. What Tomasito does and what Antonio Gades and others are doing in the theater are innovations. But so was the bulería when it was evolved little more than a century ago. So was Carmen Amaya's adoption of the man's zapateado. It was the vitality of her dancing that made it influential. Flamenco, whether sung, played, or danced, is created by its performers.

4

The Guitar and Its Music

The voice first, then rhythm . . . all the rest comes after.

PACO DE LUCÍA

The role of the guitar, at least as we know it, may be relatively recent. José Blas Vega has recorded an old storyteller. The old man goes on and on, and it might make tedious listening but for two things. The first is that his story is recognizably the fifteenth-century ballad of Gerineldo. Since he is illiterate, as his father was before him, you have to conclude that his stories have been learned by rote and handed down from father to son for up to five hundred years—and yet are still recognizably close to the original. There is nothing incredible in this: there are many examples of peoples who depend on oral tradition memorizing and passing stories on for hundreds of years. The second point of interest is that, in the middle of his story, the old man suddenly breaks into a chant and continues by singing the story. The melody is strange and modal, and very close in style to the *toná* and the *corredera* (ballad), which are the oldest known forms of flamenco—indeed, listening to this man's chanting, one might almost be tempted to say as old as Homer. The recording rather convincingly points to flamenco's origins being in the unaccompanied chanting of ballads, laments, work songs, and the like. Nobody knows when the guitar came to be added to the song. It has been

71

around since the Renaissance, but only in the last eighty years or so has it become more than a rhythmic accompaniment that gave the song an organized structure and rhythmic shape. As recently as 1990 flamenco recordings still omitted the guitarist's name. Today that has changed. Even the *martinete*, one of the few old, unaccompanied forms still sung in free rhythm, is nowadays often sung with a guitar accompaniment that puts a seguiriya rhythm to it.

For the flamenco singer, the guitar is the perfect accompanying instrument. It is percussive as well as tuneful, and so can give the song a setting of rhythmic force as well as of mood and harmony. This remains true, in spite of recent exploration of the possibilities of the flute and drums, which have come in as part of the search for roots (the flute was used in Moorish days) and for fusion with other musical fields. Even the playing of guitar solos is a fairly modern development, and more often heard outside Andalusia than in: its music is based on the song and on the accompanying falsetas the guitarist plays to introduce the song and between the verses. Furthermore, solo guitar remains flamenco only insofar as it stays faithful to the character of the song, which, as we have seen, seeks above all the dramatic expression of extreme emotion. The solo instrument either conveys this or else weaves a decorative filigree round it. Much of the difference between flamenco and classical guitar stems from this, differences both in the instrument itself and in the technique of playing it.

The flamenco guitar itself is not an offshoot from the classical instrument as played by John Williams or Julian Bream. Rather, it is the other way round: performance in the concert hall demanded more resonance and a bigger and purer tone, so classical guitars were built with deeper bodies and ever-finer fan strutting to make the face more resonant and allow the sound to carry farther. Meanwhile the neck was widened to make easier the fingering of Bach-style counterpoint. Except for the wider neck, the flamenco guitar had no need of these changes. Driving rhythms, dramatic expression,

Figure 20. The guitarist El Coquillo.

and a bright sound are more important to the flamenco player than sweetness of tone or the ability to make a plucked note carry to the back of a concert hall. So the flamenco guitar has stayed largely as it was—with a shallower body, faced with spruce (as indeed are classical guitars and all the violin family), and with sides and back of light-colored cypress, in contrast to the dark rosewood of classical guitars. (The choice of wood for the sides and back makes little difference to the sound, but cypress grows locally, while rose-wood is a more expensive import.) The neck is set to give a slightly lower action, which means that the strings are closer to the frets, are easier to press, and feel softer under the fingers. To a flamenco, the strings of a classical guitar feel hard under the fingers, especially in the rasgueados. I'm not sure, but I think this low action may also help the brightness of tone, since all Spanish-made guitars tend to give out a more generous, bright sound than do, say, the Japanese ones, which are true and pure and rounded in tone, but which tend to hold the sound back inside the body. But this Spanish quality is enhanced in the flamenco guitar. However, since Paco de Lucía many flamenco guitarists have been moving toward the concert sound. Rafael Riqueni, for example, sounds to me more like a classical than a flamenco guitarist.

I have twice had the chance to play on a concert Ramírez, which is the Rolls-Royce of concert guitars. The second occasion was when I was out with a Gypsy guitarist and his uncle, a retired dancer. We went to call on a friend of theirs, who collected guitars. When the drink, serrano ham, and cheese were on the table, our host brought out a few to show us. The guitarist made a grab for a modern Granada-made flamenco instrument; I went for the Ramírez; and, with that choice available, neither of us could quite believe the other's preference. Feeling he was among friends, the dancer started to sing. So, obviously, after a bit of chat, the Ramírez was put away. We were in for a *juerga*: the better part of a night of singing, each encouraging the others. On many such occasions, not even the guitar comes out—just song, with only palmas or knuckles for rhythm.

What I say above needs a bit of qualification. Since Paco de Lucía, many flamenco guitarists have been moving toward the concert sound. It would be hard to write on the guitar today without referring to him. He is not only a phenomenal player; he is perhaps the most important musician to come out of Spain in the last quarter of the twentieth century. There have been guitarists throughout the twentieth century whose influence was widespread and deep: Ramón Montoya, the most ground-breaking; Sabicas, who played for Carmen Amaya, and who was largely responsible for spreading appreciation of the guitar in the United States; Niño Ricardo, Paco de Lucía's early hero; even Diego del Gastor, though his lilt and poetry were almost at war with technical virtuosity, making him less influential on the younger generation. There are also other guitarists today whose virtuosity, tone, or musicianship might be compared to Paco's. Paco Peña composed a flamenco mass, founded the Córdoba guitar competition, and has produced flamenco shows that promote the music and its younger exponents, and his advice was sought by John Williams on how to play the music of Granados. Manolo Sanlúcar has composed an opera and holds his own with Paco de Lucía in the astonishing sevillanas they play as a duet for Carlos Saura's *Sevillanas*.

But of no one else can it be said that you can recognize his influence on a whole generation of guitarists. It is not only the Paco de Lucía sound: he has expanded the whole harmonic vocabulary of flamenco. Furthermore, his influence spreads far beyond flamenco. His playing of Rodrigo's *Concierto de Aranjuez* was endorsed by the composer himself; he is celebrated worldwide for the music he makes with jazz notables such as John McLaughlin and Al DiMeola; and with his own band he takes flamenco as a base to explore other sorts of music, as you can hear in Saura's film *Flamenco*. Yet in *cante jondo* he remains authentic. And the little he says shows his integrity: hence my epigraph to this chapter. For "voice and rhythm" were part of flamenco long before the guitar; in saying "all the rest comes after," he is referring to his own art.

The flamenco guitarist's playing technique differs from that of the classical player mainly in the use of the right hand. The left hand is the same, except that the flamenco player does not use a footstool or set the guitar on his left thigh, so the left wrist does not normally arch so far round under the neck. I say "normally" because the old-fashioned way of holding the guitar almost vertically did allow such a wrist position. But nowadays they hold the instrument in whatever way they find most comfortable, and nearly always on the right thigh. Perriquín, El Niño Jero, is as likely as not to hold it three different ways in the course of one song. But he learned the traditional way. His father was an itinerant singer who wanted to save money on an accompanist, so Perriquín El Niño (the child) was on the roads as a professional by the age of five. And he is still a professional at forty-something, and a very good one. Nowadays there are guitar schools, but many of the best players come out of what one might call dynasties, where they learn by imitating their elders—families such as the Moraos and Parillas of Jerez, or the Carmonas (the Habichuelas and Ketama) of Granada. I doubt whether the phenomenal Paco de Lucía ever took lessons, other than from his father. As children such people are likely to concentrate more on imitating the sounds they hear than to bother about the hand and body position.

The most characteristic difference in right-hand technique is the rasgueado, with its drum-roll rhythmic effect created by striking several strings with the back of the fingers, one after another in alternation, as against the technique of plucking the strings with the finger, which is called *picado*. This rapid drumming of the fingernails on strings in the rasgueado may sound straightforward to the outsider, a simple technique anyone could do once they had the trick. Not so. The varying demands of binary and ternary rhythms, in different tempos and conjunctions, mean that there are five or six different ways of producing rasgueado to make it fit the rhythm with that accuracy and bite that will earn the singer's or dancer's accolade, "He has good compás." Flamenco shares the plucking techniques with classical play. In both, the player can either pluck the string in an upward curving movement of the finger or else produce a bigger, singing tone by pressing down on the string so that the finger comes to rest on the next one. Curiously enough, the more exotic rasgueado technique originated in Castilian Spain; Moorish music used only the picado, and with a plectrum.

The player has various other ways of producing sounds, each creating its own particular tone or effect. The flamenco tremolo differs from the classical in that it is made up of five notes rather than four, though the effect is similar. Perhaps I should explain, for those unfamiliar with it, that in guitar music tremolo is the technique of making a melody with each note rapidly repeated. Readers may well be familiar with Tárrega's tremolo study, known as *Recuerdos de la Alhambra*, which concert players use so often as an encore. The fact that he called the piece *Memories of the Alhambra* may well be because he associated the sound with Granada, where the tremolo is such a prominent feature of the guitarist's accompaniment to the *granaína*. (I illustrate this on CD track 14). Other techniques of the flamenco player—apart from that of playing the string with the left hand (*ligado*), which he shares with the classical player—are the *alzapúa*, or use of the thumbnail as an upward-moving plectrum, and some purely rhythmic effects made by playing on strings while they are muted by the left hand, and by tapping the face of the guitar while playing the strings (all flamenco guitars have a plate on the face as protection from the players' fingernails.) Together, these and other techniques enable the player to provide the rhythmic variety and force, and the sometimes explosive tone, that make his music flamenco.

Having said that, it should be added that the guitar often gives a lilting and lyrical setting to the drama of the song. Listen to a soleá (CD track 4 or 5) and compare it to a seguiriya (CD track 2). Someone has described the seguiriya as "a cry of despair" in contrast to the soleá's "stoic resignation." It seems to me that the guitar contributes to this: the guitarist's falsetas to the seguiriya accentuate its rhythms with dark, punched chords, thought to evoke the tolling of the death knell, while there is a touch of elegiac sweetness to the falsetas of the soleá. What is more, with the guitar, as with the dance, there are no rules: the music is valid or not, depending on the quality of the player. The music played by Gerardo Nuñez in his Madrid nightclub, the Gallo Azul, is like no other you have ever heard. But it is flamenco.

In a parallel way, this marriage of tradition and innovation that characterizes any "traditional" art applies to the falsetas. There are themes and turns of phrase particular to each song form. Each must have started when one player invented his own, which pleased others and was copied. But to be influential, the innovator has to be traditional too. Ramón Montoya's younger relative, Carlos, was a virtuoso, and made a fortune in the United States. He could not have done so in Andalusia, where he was held in contempt—for, as the recordings show, he allowed self-indulgence to come before fidelity to the compás. The marriage of tradition and innovation also appears in a shorter time span within the development of a single guitarist. When I first heard Antonio Jero, for example, he played with good compás but with simple and traditional falsetas. Five years later he is using harmonies of modern classical music such as did not exist before Igor Stravinsky.

The flamenco guitar is more familiar to us than the song or dance, and its music needs less explaining. There may also be guitarists among the readers. So, in the next three paragraphs, I write with them in mind as well as the general reader. This entails occasionally getting a wee bit technical and you may want to skip them.

There is need to explain a bit more about the Andalusian mode, or E mode, which I shall do here because it closely concerns the guitar. We have already seen that the tunes seem difficult to us, partly because of the singer's vocal wanderings but also because the scale is different from ours. It is in fact a variety of the old Phrygian mode of medieval plainchant, which runs up the white keys of the piano (the so-called natural notes) from E to E. Our major and minor scales are simply two other modes, formed by running up the white keys from C to C and from A to A, respectively; these were adopted later, when harmony evolved, and they came to dominate all Western music because they lend themselves more readily to harmonization than other modes do. The guitar gives harmonic shape to the *cante* (which is the word used for flamenco song, in distinction to other forms of song, which are called *canto*). So it is not surprising that a lot of cante has moved in the direction of the easily harmonizable major or minor, only falling at the end from C (major) or A (minor) down through G to the Andalusian final cadence. This cadence, or ending of a piece of music, is different from what we are used to. We saw in chapter 2 that in our Western music, you can hear that a tune in C is coming to a close when you hear it move from a G chord to a final C. But the flamenco knows he is coming to the end when he hears not G and then C, but the chords on F and then E. The guitarist plays the F major chord, then slides his fingers back one fret to produce the E major chord, and this tells the listener that the song is ended. I shall refer to this cadence pattern as F–E.

If you look at the scale from E to E, you will see that flamenco tunes that sound as if they are in C major or A minor use mainly the upper half of this scale. But the old seguiriya stays mainly in the lower part of the E scale, uninfluenced by modern tunes or Western harmony. The folk fandangos such as the *verdiales*, which were flamencoized in the later nineteenth century, may sound unfamiliar to us in their melodies, but they are based on the tonic and dominant harmonies of our major scale. The *cantiñas*, which also came into flamenco in the nineteenth century, some of them from operettas and popular songs, are even more determinedly major in their tunes.

The flamenco scale differs from the old Phrygian mode in one or two ways. The guitar uses the chord of E major (E–G-sharp–B), when the natural notes of the white piano keys would give E–G–B, a minor chord. If you add this one to the common chords obtainable on the white keys of the piano, you find that the guitarist has five chords at his disposal: C major (C–E–G), A minor (A–C–E), G major (G–B–D), and F major (F–A–C), and the above-mentioned E major (E–G-sharp–B). (He also has those of D minor and E minor, but seldom uses the latter in the E mode.) Sometimes the singer will also use the G-sharp. In the tiento, for example, the tune tends to rise via G-sharp and come down via G-natural. Very occasionally you will hear the jump from G-sharp to F-natural, an interval of a tone and a half. It gives to the song a tang of exotic spice—not surprisingly, since it is a characteristic of Arab and Jewish music. But to be good, it has to be occasional, for with flamenco as with cookery, a little spice enhances the dish. Use too much and you spoil it.

There are other incidental differences from the old E mode, such as the singer's use of B-flat, mainly in songs that derive from the fandango. I imagine that this melodic touch grew out of the harmonies: in the first two lines of the fandango the guitar moves from C to the F major chord, which would naturally pull the singer toward a B-flat. If you do not happen to have learned the language of music, this discussion of G-sharps and B-flats may make hard reading; and my saying that the singer would "naturally" use a B-flat might seem almost insulting. But please believe that you would *hear* these points at once. Try, for example, having someone play the three chords C major, C7, and F major: the middle one, which is simply C major with an added B-flat, seems to pull you into the F major. Details such as these seem to me to show the influence the guitar has had on the old modal songs, by its use of harmonies drawn from our Western major and minor scales. I give more detail in the next chapter on the song forms. Here, as ever, for convenience, I have described the music as if it were always in the key of (modal) E. The flamenco guitarist uses a capodaster (*cejilla*), which he clips onto the neck of the guitar, in order to change the real key to whatever suits the pitch of the singer's voice. Thereafter he plays almost always in one of two positions. Without the capo, these would be either E, which he calls *por arriba*, or A, which he calls *en medio*.

For all the guitar's importance, one of the most surprising things about it has been its anonymity—at least until recently, and except for a few stars. Only in recordings of the last dozen years or so has anyone bothered to add the guitarist's name to that of the singer. And though the convention, at the end of a song, is for the singer to make a gesture of sharing the applause, until recently you had the impression that it was a formality, while the dancer sometimes did not even go that far. Of course the accompanist is subservient to the singer, just as a piano accompanist is, but his is a highly skilled art. So it pleased me to hear a flamenco agree. I was talking with the dancer La Presi, who had been working in a tourist tablao.

> *RT*: Juan told me that when he's playing, it's the singer who must lead. He must give the singer something to feed on, but he must follow him. That's what he says his performance depends on: he cannot play well if the singer is in poor form.

> *La Presi*: The guitarist has the most difficult job of the three, because a good guitarist can have a bad dancer, out of compás, and he will be disastrous, no matter how good he is—even Paco de Lucía. Yet a dancer, if she's dominating the rhythm, she can work with someone playing a can. . . . Some dancers get very irritated with guitarists, and they speak badly of them if they can't do what they are supposed to do. They have to keep in mind that the guitarist's job is very difficult. I respect the guitarists. Even if they are bad, I try to keep my papers together—it's a very difficult instrument.

For me, the most surprising aspect of the flamenco guitar is the sheer virtuosity of so many of the players. As I have already suggested, apropos of Diego del Gastor, this widespread virtuosity carries its own dangers, for it is easier to emulate cleverness than art. If you saw the Irish show *Riverdance*, you will have heard Rafael Riqueni, who has all the skills as well as something of the sound of a classical guitarist. When the music requires brilliance, he shines. But I have also heard him wreck an otherwise haunting performance of that saddest and simplest of songs, the *Malagueña* of La Trini (I quote the words in chapter 5). His falsetas in it were a brilliant display and utterly inappropriate. He is one of the vast majority of players influenced by Paco de Lucía. But it would be unfair to blame this influence for not going with the same art or integrity. I will end with another example. Diego del Morao is in

81

his early twenties. His father, the great Moraíto, claims he is already passed in skill by his son. His great uncle, the equally great Morao, is reticent about him. Both facts suggest a young player among the many who put showing off their skill before good flamenco. But I have heard him do the opposite. He was accompanying the young Carmen Grilo in a recital at a big festival. She has a movingly good flamenco voice and is appreciated in her hometown, but she had yet to hit the headlines elsewhere—and she was feeling ill with a bad cold for this, her big chance. Diego put all his skill and concentration into helping her by good accompaniment and good flamenco, with never a sign of display for himself. True artistry is never common, and some of today's finest artists (such as Vicente Amigo) are heading for a music I don't like, but I see no cause to worry for the future.

5

The Song Forms

There is a firm belief that flamenco cannot be explained. "If you don't feel it *here*" (hand on heart, eyes rolled heavenward) "no explanation can help!" A cop-out if ever I heard one. I was much encouraged to discover that the fine flamenco singer Calixto Sánchez agreed. "You can help people to get further inside the flamenco world," he said, "put the various forms and rhythms of flamenco within people's reach. You can't teach them the art, but you can show them all its ingredients."

I am convinced that we who have not been hearing it all our lives can be helped to enjoy the song if we can hear what lies, as it were, inside it. We then not only recognize it, but are able to begin to appreciate what the singer is doing to it. Mere explanation doesn't help, since words cannot convey music. So what follows is meant to accompany a hearing of the recorded examples on the accompanying CD, whose contents are listed in appendix 5. This chapter is intended for reference as much as for reading, but I put it at the heart of the book because it is my main reason for writing this guide.

When we listen to music we tend to hear the tune first, and only then, perhaps, the harmony, rhythm, and words. To the flamenco, the tune is little or nothing, and the harmony less. He is aware, above all, of the words and their rhythmic and forceful expression. In any case, with the oldest forms—those that used to be called *cante jondo* or deep song—the tune is so basic as hardly to count: it consists of rising or falling by steps through four or five notes.

So the tune, as you might write it down, is not flamenco. This is not merely because it omits the singer's melodic weavings and his use of quarter tones, but because it cuts out what matters: the words, rhythmic force, tone of voice, and expression. It also omits what is less obvious, namely, that he constantly hits the note just off the beat, early or late. The effect of this is to give his song a seamless, curving character. It is held together by the guitar's steadiness, and by the listener's own awareness of the underlying measure. By the singer's awareness, too—for however freely he seems to treat the rhythm, you could take a metronome to a long song and not catch him out. This is why this point remains true, even for a singer *pa' atrás*, that is to say, one who sings for a dancer and so must above all give her a reliable rhythmic base. *Tiene buen compás* (he has good rhythm) is the dancer's highest praise for a singer.

You may have noticed I said that the art *used* to be called cante jondo. The words *jondo* and *jondura* are still used (they are the Gypsy pronunciation of the Spanish words *hondo* and *hondura*: "deep," "depth"). But *cante jondo* in the days of Manuel de Falla and García Lorca was used to describe the real thing as against *flamenco*—a word they used in contempt to refer to frivolous trivia. Nowadays *jondura* is applied not to this or that song form, but to the way it is sung. Tomasa La Macanita, singing the supposedly festive bulerías, can move her audience more strongly than a lesser singer performing a tragic siguiriya. And today the word *flamenco* covers the whole art.

A song puts music to *words*. Some people go to the opera without knowing what the singer is going on about, and some listen to lieder without understanding the words. But they are cutting themselves off from a crucial part of it. The flamenco singer recreates and embroiders the song form in the way he does in order to express what the words mean for him. So, in most cases, I add a selection of words so as to give you at least a taste of the song's meaning or mood.

I refer to all the pieces as if they are in the E mode, whatever the actual pitch the performers decide on, and irrespective of whether the guitarist plays in the hand position for E (*por arriba*) or for A (*en medio*). I mention it where songs are always played in one or the other position, as well as the rare special cases in which I feel the tunes must be given in that key, which will be either modal B (one sharp) for the granaína, or F-sharp (two sharps) for the Levant songs.

There are upward of fifty palos, which I group here as follows:

+ Tonás: tonás, martinetes, carceleras, deblas, and romances. Track 1
+ Siguiriyas, livianas, and serranas. Tracks 2 and 3
+ Soleares, including alboreás and soleares por bulería. Tracks 4 and 5
+ Bulerías. Track 6
+ Tangos, tientos, and tanguillos. Track 7
+ Cantiñas: alegrías, caracoles, mirabrás, romeras, and rosas. Track 8
+ Polo and caña
+ Peteneras. Track 9
+ The fandango family: verdiales, fandangos locales, fandangos de Huelva, rondeñas, malagueñas, jaberas, fandangos personales or fandangos grandes, and granaínas. Tracks 10–15
+ Cantes de Levante: tarantas, tarantos, mineras, cartageneras, and others. Tracks 16 and 17
+ Farruca and garrotín. Tracks 18 and 19
+ Cantes de ida y vuelta: guajiras, rumbas, milongas, and colombianas. Track 20
+ Zambras: zambras, alboreás, moscas, and cachuchas
+ Songs influenced by flamenco: saetas, villancicos, sevillanas, campanilleros, bamberas, nanas, pregones, temporeras, and cantes de trilla. Track 21

Chapter 5

Clearly, a single CD cannot cope with even half of these, so I have recorded the ones you are most likely to hear. While my first aim has been to illustrate the song form, I have also tried to include songs from a variety of sources and occasions. To reproduce only the great and famous such as you can hear on most CDs would not show flamenco as it is lived by flamencos, whoever and wherever. So the artistry varies. Not all the performances are brilliant, but the songs cover the spectrum, and they are alive.

✦ Tonás: tonás, martinetes, carceleras, deblas, and romances
Track 1

Tonás are the oldest flamenco songs and the least commercial ones. They probably grew out of the ballads (*romances* or *corridos*). They are, or should be, sung unaccompanied. But they are coming back into common use and, as usual, the dancers' perpetual search for new forms has led to some of these songs' being accompanied and therefore in rhythm. So you hear martinetes performed to the sound of hammer on anvil beating a siguiriya rhythm, and romances to guitar accompaniment in soleá rhythm (I give the rhythms under those song forms). Strangely, these purest of songs, though they may sound weird to us, are mostly not in the flamenco E mode but in the major keys of Western music. That is to say, they start and return to C, not to E.

Toná is the general term and is used to name any that are not martinetes, carceleras, or deblas.

Martinetes are songs of the smithy—hence the sound of hammer on anvil referred to above. The "tune" consists of a rise up four notes of the scale and down again—nearly always in the major (C–D–E–F–E–D–C), but I have heard them in the minor (A–B–C–D–C–B–A) and in the Andalusian mode (E–F–G–A–G–F–E). They are the ones you are most likely to hear. The differences in tune between them and other tonás are so slight you would have to be an expert to recognize them.

Although the words came from the smithy, they are not specifically about it. There is no special theme.

Desgraciaíto aquél	He's an unhappy man
que come pan de mano ajena	who lives on another's bread
siempre mirando a la carita	always looking at his face
si la ponen mala o buena.	to see what mood he's in.
A mí me llaman el loco	They call me the crazy man
porque siempre voy callao:	because I never speak:
llamarme poquito a poco	call me "softly softly,"
que soy un loco de cuidado.	I'm crazy by caution.
Si la mamaíta mía de mis entrañas	If the mother of my heart
levantara su cabeza	looked up and saw me
y me viera como me veo	as I see myself
se moriría de tristeza	she would die of sorrow.

Carceleras are prison songs. Except for the words (prison being the only theme) they are like other tonás, differing from the martinete only in the way the voice drops (to G) at the end of the phrase. I have only heard them twice in the last six years. They were not even used for the 1999 song contest organized for prisoners of the Andalusian jails and won by Dolores Agujetas's brother Antonio Agujetas Hijo, who was doing a stretch for putting a knife into a passer-by who did not want to give him his wallet. The need to get money for drugs is the commonest cause of crime today. The problem affects Gypsy and *gachó* alike, but for the Gypsy, drugs seem to have replaced persecution as the main source of tragedy. And perhaps the worse because traditionally his main source of happiness has been his family, his freedom, and sunlight—all cut off by imprisonment.

Andame los pasos, mare,	Do what is needed, mother,
que me saquen de aquí	to get me out of here.
que me tienen a mí encerraito	They've got me locked in
por lo que no cometí.	for something I didn't do.

(This is as good a place as any to point to the Andalusian habit of making almost any word a diminutive: *encerrado* [locked up] has nothing charming or small about it that it should become *encerra(d)ito*.)

Deblas disappeared and were not so much revived as reconstituted. They are even rarer than carceleras and sung at the top of the vocal range, like a *macho* to other tonás. The *macho* is a way of ending a song, usually by raising the pitch, sometimes by singing faster.

Romances (ballads) are a form of toná. Nowadays, when done with guitar it is usually played in soleá rhythm. Furthermore, it is likely to be from Federico García Lorca's *Romancero Gitano* (Gypsy Ballad Book). García Lorca has become a sort of god of flamenco, despite the fact that his portrayal of Gypsies belongs more to romantic imagination than reality. During his centenary I heard someone comment: "If García Lorca heard what they are saying about him this year, he'd shoot *himself.*"

The singer of the toná on track 1, Dolores Agujeta, is the daughter of the great Manuel Agujetas—spellings of the name vary—whose martinete is the best thing in Carlos Saura's film *Flamenco* (see appendix 2 for details). Like all her family, she is a creature of impulse and instinct, rather than reason and control. Going to lunch with her means hordes of children and in-laws, gusts of laughter, and the occasional squall, not to mention dogs, hens, and the family pig. It also means you sit down to a (very good) lunch by five o'clock in the afternoon and do not get up until eight. You don't get singing any more Gypsy than hers.

Figure 21. Dolores Agujeta, singer.
She can be heard on the accompanying CD,
tracks 1 and 12.

✦ Siguiriyas, livianas, and serranas
Tracks 2 and 3

The **siguiriya** is the heart of deep song. It expresses anguish, lament, and despair, and has been described as an outcry against fate and the quintessence of tragic song. It is also the most indisputably Gypsy of the song forms, which is relevant because the history of the Gypsies *is* fundamentally tragic—the tragedy of a people who stick to their own customs and laws in the face of the laws and customs of the land they come to live in. Thus their history of persecution is the more tragic for their having to some extent brought it on themselves.

All the signs are that the song is ancient in origin. The tune of this most fundamental of all flamenco cantes is also the most basic: a descent of four notes down the scale, A–G–F–E. You will hear many variations on this, but this is its heart. All the rest is created by the singer. What this means is not that the siguiriya is the easiest palo to understand or to sing, but the contrary: it is the most difficult. Perhaps more than with any other, the singer creates the song. He has to create its musical shape, and above all, he has to fill that shape with powerful feeling. The need to find the intense feeling inside himself often gives him the urge to sing another song first in order to prepare for it, nowadays often a *fandango grande* (discussed later in this chapter).

The siguiriya is most clearly characterized by its distinctive rhythm, slow, heavy and insistent:

$$\mathsf{I \,.\, I \,.\, I \,.\, .\, I \,.\, .\, I \,.}$$

Paco Peña associates it with the sound of the death knell, which is appropriate, since it was once called the *playera*, which means keening or mourning. And the dancer Mario Maya, in his staging of de Falla's *El amor brujo*, used it with chilling effect, quietly stamped out by the dancers' feet, to represent death.

The song of the siguiriya is woven round a basic tune made up of a descending scale from A to E and ending with a monotone on E. (I am here referring to the Andalusian mode as if all songs were pitched to E). Among the many strange features of the siguiriya, one is that nobody is quite sure (not even the composer Manuel de Falla) what the singer's rhythm or time signature is. Most tend to agree that he sings in approximately 7/8 time. Another is that the key words at the end of the phrase are thrown away, as it were, on a quiet monotone. In this alone the siguiriya relates to Gypsy singing in other parts of the world, Romania for instance. A French researcher has called it "occultation" and thinks it has to do with the Gypsies' status as outcasts. He may be right.

The guitar is in compás, or strict rhythm, with a twelve-count of

$$1\ 2\ 3\ 4\ 5\ 6\ 7\ 8\ 9\ 10\ 11\ 12$$

You hear him punch this rhythm out in chords on A–G–F–E on the accented beats (1, 3, 5, 8, 11). In this case the pitch is bound to be different because the guitarist always plays the siguiriya *en medio*—that is, as though for the key of A, wherever he may put his capodaster.

The siguiriya was not danced until the first half of the twentieth century, when it became one of the earlier victims of the dancers' perpetual search for new forms. In this it contrasts with the soleá, that other form at the heart of flamenco song, which has been danced for as long as we have any record.

Palmas are used only when the siguiriya is danced. When the siguiriya is sung *a palo seco*, the rhythm is usually tapped out with a stick or with knuckles, or with the palm of the hand, as in track 3.

The remate (way of finishing the song) is often done by a last verse in the major mode, called a *macho*, or *cabales*, or else with one line in the major (called *de cambio*) before reverting to the flamenco E mode. Note that anything in the major is going to be sung at the upper half of the scale, since a tune in C (major) is at the top end of the E mode.

The name *siguiriya* is a Gypsy deformation of the word *seguidilla*, which is a Spanish verse form of four lines of seven and five syllables alternating. But the verse has varied in the siguiriya, and the music has no connection with the Spanish seguidilla. The siguiriya traditionally lengthens the third line to make seven, five, eleven, and five syllables, though today you may well find it sung to other verse forms. Don't worry about spellings: the Spanish *seguidilla* comes from *seguir* (to follow) and is so spelled; but *siguiriya* is often spelled *seguiriya*.

The first siguiriya below I've heard in Spanish and Caló, so I give both versions.

Anguish

Penas tiene mi mare	My mother has her troubles
penas tengo yo	and I have mine
y las que siento son las de mi mare	my mother's are the ones I feel
que las mías no.	not my own.

Ducas tenela min dai
ducas tenelo yo
las de min dai yo siento
las de mangue no.

Love

Cuando yo me muera	When I die
te pido un encargo;	I ask you a favor:
que con las trenzas de tu pelo negro	bind my hands together
me amarres mis manos.	in the locks of your long black hair

Prison

A la luna le pío	I beg the moon
la del alto cielo	up there in the sky
como le pío que le sacan a mi pare	I beg it to get my father out
de donde está metío.	from where they've put him.

Death

Pal hospital yo me voy,	I'm going to the hospital,
por Dios, compañera,	for God's sake, companion,
pa no dejarte morirte sola	I won't let you die alone:
me voy a tu vera.	I'm going with you.

Some very old words have survived. The following dates from about two hundred years ago, possibly when an epidemic was blamed on the Gypsies.

Los jerás por las esquinas	The gentlemen round the corner
con velones y faról	with lamps and lanterns
en voz alta se decían	came shouting
marrarlo que es calorró.	kill him: he's a Gypsy.

The siguiriya on track 2 is sung by the great siguiriyero Antonio Nuñez ("Chocolate"), accompanied by Diego Amaya, and quoted by kind permission of Manuel Morao and Gitanos de Jerez from the album *Evocación de Terremoto*. This is only an extract though, traditionally, it is a whole siguiriya for, properly speaking, a siguiriya consists of a single verse of four lines. Nowadays, with commercial recordings and public performances, several verses are usually sung; the original track of this lasts seven minutes.

Track 3 is a *siguiriya a palo seco* (unaccompanied siguiriya) sung by Antonio El Monea.

The day I recorded the siguiriya on track 3, we had been jolted by the sudden death of the club barman Luciano, a simple, kindly man of forty, of whom we were all fond. In the evening Antonio came round, bringing three Japanese. I put out beer and manchego cheese, and we sat around the table. Why the massive popularity of flamenco among the Japanese? There are perhaps more enthusiasts in that country than in the rest of the world together. They have at least two magazines, one of which publishes ten thousand copies, and the classes given by famous dancers in the Amor de Dios studios in Madrid may have as many as seventeen Japanese students out of twenty. I had thought the answer must lie in their culture, which inhibits the outward expression of emotion. Flamenco stresses the strong expression of it and so, as an art form, it would give them a legitimate outlet. A Japanese acquaintance said he thought this was only part of the answer and didn't elaborate. During this siguiriya, one of the guests sat listening, her face impassive. But her eyes filled with tears. Antonio sang and Emi wept. "I didn't understand the words," she said, "but his singing made me think of Luciano." Antonio had sung of grief for the death of a mother. So now I think Emi's tears suggest a deeper affinity.

I put the livianas and serranas in this group because these two song forms follow the compás of the siguiriya

⎸.⎸.⎸..⎸..⎸.

—but they might be described as watered-down versions, as well as slightly faster. They resemble one another but, curiously they seem to do so, coming from opposite ends: the liviana sounds as though it developed from the siguiriya, while the serrana clearly has its origins in folk song.

The **liviana** originates in Puerto Real, a small town on the bay of Cádiz. The Spanish word means "frivolous," which it isn't. It is sung to the siguiriya rhythm and at one time was used by singers as a way of leading into the intensity of the siguiriya, so perhaps it takes its name from *liviana*'s other meaning: a lead mule. Nowadays, singers who don't want to tackle from cold the extreme demands of the siguiriya commonly use the fandango grande as a warm-up. And until recently, it had become rare. But in today's world of instant communication, fashion affects flamencos as it does anyone else, and both forms are coming back.

The tune stays within the six notes of the E mode. It runs up the scale from E to C and back down again. The second phrase is similar to that of the first *ayes* of the caña, rising and falling by only three notes and equivalent to the throwaway monotone that ends any line of the siguiriya. The tune then repeats the first phrase, except that it comes back down to a pause on a G major chord before returning to the E. Thus the whole song stays within this limited compass unless it is ended by a *macho*, in which case the first phrase goes up a whole octave, while otherwise following the tune described above.

The guitar usually plays *en medio* as for a siguiriya but with less death-knell insistence, and often making the last four chords a simple descent from A to E. The words follow the verse form of the (Castilian) seguidilla: a four-line verse followed by three lines with changed assonance, all lines alternating between seven and five syllables. This is no rigid rule: you also hear *coplas* (as in the first four lines below) and the true siguiriya form of four lines with seven, five, eleven, and five syllables, as in the *macho* below.

Yo me paso las noches	I spend my nights
sin coger sueño . . .	without sleep . . .
si vienen a buscarme	if they come to get me
¿dónde me meto?	where can I hide?
Como quien dice	As you might say
acorralao, y no tengo	cornered
salía posible.	and no way out.

Mú poquito se ha dicho	Little gets said
de los cobardes	about cowards
yo me defiendo sólo	I just defend myself
de quien se encarte.	from those who get in my way.
Navaja y tralla	Knife and lash
yo paso por las buenas	I carry on through
y por las malas.	good times and bad.

Macho

La corná del tiempo	I've been gored
llevo yo en mis carnes	by the horns of Time;
la trica, trisé (mare de mi alma, ay)	exploitation, O mother mine,
con el tiempo sale.	I've seen it all.

Chapter 5

The word **serrana** means "from the mountains" (*sierras*). Which mountains depends on where you come from: the province of Córdoba with its Sierra Morena, the province of Cádiz with its Serranía de Ronda, or any of the mountainous eastern provinces. The serrana started life as folk song, and when flamencoized in the nineteenth century it came to be sung to a siguiriya rhythm. This is curious, because its themes are always of country life, and the words are often sentimental. Musically it is like a bigger version of the liviana, for it ranges over a full octave with long-held high notes, and it demands good breath control, especially at the song's most characteristic and unmistakable moment: a long, slow rise through the octave, singing in triplets. Both liviana and serrana have a siguiriya rhythm; both use the same verse form; both have been rare, though the serrana, being danced, is heard slightly more often. Having stressed its folk-song origins, I should also make clear that a good singer can make it sound as flamenco as any.

The shape of the tune echoes that of the liviana, except in two places. The singer starts with a long held note at the top of the scale and comes down pausing on the C and on down to the low E. His second phrase echoes that of the liviana (and of the *ayes* in the caña and polo); and his repeat of the first phrase comes down to a G, as in the liviana (and, incidentally, the soleá, too). The main difference lies in the wide vocal range and in that slow rise through the octave.

The guitar is played *por arriba* (in the position for E), which it never is for the siguiriya, and it has a more melodious accompaniment compared to the heavy, punched chords of the siguiriya.

The dance, like the music, tends less toward flamenco bite (*pellizco*) than toward gracefulness and is often done in "typical" (that is, picturesque) peasant dress, often with the conical Cordobese hat of tradition.

The words follow the same verse form as the liviana:

En la sierra de Ronda	In the Ronda mountains
hay una ventera	there's an innkeeping girl
ella sola perfuma	she's so sweet she perfumes
la sierra entera.	the whole mountain range.
Es tan bonita	She's so pretty
que en la sierra la llaman	in the mountains they call her
la virgencita.	the little virgin.

Less mawkish is this older one:

Venta de Viveros	The inn at Viveros
dichoso sitio	is a happy place
si es cristiano el ventero	for the innkeeper is a Christian
y es moro el vino.	and the wine is Moorish.
Sitio dichoso	The place is fine
si el ventero es cristiano	with a Christian for an innkeeper
y el vino es moro.	and Moorish wine.

I quote these two verses because they are known to be traditional. It is often difficult to tell whether a song's words have been composed by writers pretending to authenticity. This is particularly true of the serrana, whose words often harp on how glad the singer is to be a bandit or a smuggler—too often for me to believe their authenticity.

✦ **Soleares, including alboreás and soleares por bulería**
Tracks 4 and 5

As song, the **soleá** lies at the heart of flamenco, together with the siguiriya and the toná. As dance, it stands alone—at least for women, as I explain in chapter 3. Since men don't commonly dance it, it might be fairer to say that it stands at the head of the trio of soleá, alegrías, and bulerías as the leading dance forms.

There are many variants on the song according to origin—soleares from Triana, Alcalá, Utrera, Cádiz ("de Mellizo"), Jerez ("de Juaniquí"), and so on, tracks 4 and 5 being *soleares de Alcalá*. But I shall not attempt to differentiate them, because the differences are of tune only, not rhythm. The differences that do matter for us are between the soleá sung for itself and that sung for dancers.

The soleá sung for dancers switches between slow and fast (stemming, so I am told, from Arab influence). The fast sections correspond to the zapateado. In these fast bits you sometimes hear the singer leaving the soleá tune to sing a rapid series of *te quieros*, or else they are done by guitarists alone, playing with muted strings to produce a sort of brush-drum effect.

The rhythm for all soleares follows the twelve-count of

$$. . | . . | . | . | . |$$

Of these, the last two are usually silent, making a pause thus:

$$1\ 2\ \textbf{3}\ \ 4\ 5\ \textbf{6}\ \ 7\ \textbf{8}\ \ \textbf{9}\ \textbf{10}\ (11\ 12)$$

This underlying rhythm is mainly to be perceived in the dance. The guitarist plays it more as if it were in 6/8 + 3/4 time, that is,

$$| . . | . . | . | | (- -)$$

while for the singer the twelve-count acts more as an overall structure for his words and his singing. So the result is a overlay of rhythms within a complex structure.

The guitar amost always plays in the position for E (*por arriba*). His falsetas make a lilting contrast to the austere force of the song. In track 4, Melchor de Marchena's falsetas show this better than words can do: they are like a model from which others diverge to create their own.

The words may be in three- or four-line verses. Their themes are similar to those of the siguiriyas, though usually less intensely tragic.

The first soleá on the CD (track 4) is sung by José Menese, with Melchor de Marchena on guitar. It is taken from the album *Cantes flamencos básicos* with the permission of BMG Music, Spain. In this chapter I try where I can to use each song form to introduce a different aspect of flamenco. Thus for the taranta I give an example of solo guitar, in the granaína I illustrate the difference between Gypsy and non-Gypsy style, and so on. I chose this example of a soleá because both the singer and the guitarist give a wonderfully clear illustration of the form. There are more passionate performances, but this one shows the basis on which others work, and it prompts me to show the musical structure of the song. I suggest that the next bit be read while listening to track 4, with your finger on the pause button.

After the opening falsetas and the singer's *ayes* (used partly to get himself into the mood, partly to get the pitch), the singer opens with a four-line verse:

Malas lenguas van diciendo   The gossips are saying
que tú no cameles a naide   that you don't love anyone
cuando sé que por mis huesos   when I know that your desire for me
tú andas perdiendo carnes.   is wasting you away.

The first two lines are sung rising from E to A via the G-sharp of the major scale, and coming down via the G-natural of the flamenco mode. Then we hear four bars of falsetas from the guitarist. The couplet is repeated. Lines three and four follow a similar pattern but with the variation that the rise and fall of the voice both happen within line three alone. There is also a slight change of tune as the singer dwells on G while the guitar plays a C major chord, which is not heard elsewhere. The change is slight but perceptible and happens in all soleares. Line four repeats the descent from A to E. The couplet is repeated. Falsetas follow, as they do between every verse.

Hijiste cruz pa' perderme	You made the sign of the cross
	to drive me away
y al echarla te olviaste	and in doing so you forgot
que el que firma es el que pierde.	the saying "signers, losers."

In this three-line verse the repetitions are slightly changed, with the first line sung alone and the other two repeated. The song's increasing intensity makes the singer begin to go higher up the scale than previously. The last two lines follow the tune they had in the first verse, something that tends to happen in all verses.

No me llames a tu lado	Don't ask me to come back to you
si ya no valgo lo que valía	for I'm no longer the man I was
si el tiempo admitiera vuelta	if time could be turned round
que ya pasito pa' atrás daría	I would already have gone back.

Here the pathos of the words emerges with the singer staying up on the first line, as though stuck there (the guitar brings the tune back down again). He then, as it were, tries again, this time running straight on to the second line and bringing the tune back down. Instead of repeating the couplet, he twice repeats the painful second line "I'm no longer the man I was."

Dicen que yo a ti no te hablo	They say I don't speak to you
porque no terelaba valor	because I didn't have the guts
pa' tomar esa murallita	to break down the wall
que tu madre levantó	your mother raised against me.

With this verse the song hits its high point, starting almost an octave above the others and staying up until the second line brings it down. Once again, instead of repeating the couplet he dwells repeatedly on the hurtful "because I didn't have the guts"—with the added touch that on the repeats it becomes "because I *don't* have the guts" (*no terelo . . . no tengo yo valor*).

La luna tiene un menguante	The moon has its waning
lo que pue' tener mi querer,	and so can my love wane,
serrana, hasta olvidarte.	girl, until you are forgotten.

Here he repeats the first line, and in the repeat his voice goes up high and wanders around before coming down to finish the first half of the tune. The final couplet is repeated as usual, but only as to the words: he sings it the first time with a repeated falling cadence that conveys his rejection and his dejection. Then comes one last outburst at the top of his voice before again falling twice in a dying cadence on the words "until I forget you."

This is José Menese's way of singing *these* words on *this* occasion. He would never repeat it exactly, even when singing the same words: he is singing not a *soleá* but *por soleá*, within the framework of the *soleá* form.

My description is an attempt, perhaps a forlorn one, to convey in words the shape of the song's music—complicated, expressive, and artistically subtle. In the section on the fandango I point to the special skills of oral poetry; here I hope to show that the song is music whose primitive force can mask artistic sophistication. *Ojalá.*

A footnote on the language: *camelar* (love) and *terelar* (have) are Caló words; *naide* is the Gypsy way of saying *nadie*, and *serrana* is commonly used in flamenco for girl—some people assume it means a girl from the hills (*sierras*), but it is widely used for girls of whatever origin, so it may come from an Arabic word for girl, *charrana.*

José Menese is an artist of long standing, and track 4 showed his artistry. The second soléa on the CD (track 5) is performed by the brothers David and Alfredo Lagos. They are both already *figuras* (stars), though David broke through only as recently as 2000–2001 to the status that puts him in constant demand. I said of Menese's soleá that "there are more passionate performances." I prefer this one: it illustrates Paco de Lucía's "voice and rhythm—and the rest afterwards," for here the quality of David's voice bring expression and conviction to the fore. This is more remarkable because he recorded it one morning, which is not the best time of day for passionate singing, when he heard I was having difficulties getting permission to quote.

The **alboreá** is the Gypsy wedding song, also called the *albolá* (and, in Sacromonte, the *roás*). It is sung in the soleá compás, but with a more upbeat tune usually in the major, and at a brisker pace—more like a *soleá por bulería*. My source of information is José Guardia, a lawyer and flamencologist from Pinos Puente near Granada who was brought up among Gypsies and of whom a local Gypsy said to me, "You listen to Pepe—he knows." So I think the following is reasonably authoritative.

The alboreá is ritually sung and danced at Gypsy weddings. If non-Gypsies—gachés (often wrongly called payos)—have been invited, they will be asked to leave during this part of the wedding. The reason takes us into the world of the anthropologist. Each village will usually have a woman, called the *mataora*, usually old, who has a job and skill as specialized as that of the midwife: before the actual marriage, she goes to the bride's room and breaks her hymen with her hand, which is covered with a white handkerchief. With a push-and-twist motion of the two knuckles of her middle finger and the main knuckle of her third finger, three spots of blood stain the handkerchief in a triangle shape. She then comes out to display the white handkerchief with its three red stains. The girl is proven a virgin, and the wedding can go ahead. There is general relief and jubilation, and tensions are released in this dance. Who would be a girl? Or at any rate, a Gypsy girl?

En un praíto verde	In a green meadow
tendí mi pañuelo	I laid out my handkerchief
me salieron tres rosas	three roses appeared
como tres luceros.	like three evening stars.
Se logró la boda	The wedding has succeeded
que boda tan bella	what a fine wedding
que un Dibé bendijo	a God has blessed
a tan bonita estrella.	such a pretty star.

Of course you won't see or hear a live performance of this. The more traditional Gypsies are outraged that the song should have been recorded, and by their own kind. Nonetheless, there are several recorded versions of the alboreá. What you may well come across, and often, is the image of red roses on a white cloth. De Falla's song "El Paño Moruno," which uses a similar idea, has been well known abroad since Victoria de los Angeles recorded it many years ago.

Attitudes are changing. I know at least two Gypsies who have lived together as partners and had children, with no more (apparent) fallout than you would encounter in any other family. But I also know the ritual is still performed. A couple of years ago a Spanish photographer persuaded a family in Barcelona to let her photograph the wedding—including the mataora's part in it.

Essentially a slowed-down bulería, the **soleá por bulería** is an amalgam of both forms. From the bulería it takes the twelve-count that starts on 12. From the soleá it takes the melody and the guitar falsetas. Thus, rhythmically it sounds like a slow bulería; in other ways it sounds like a speeded-up soleá. Likewise, the words are less intense than those of the soleá and less pungent than the bulería's.

✦ Bulerías
Track 6

The bulería is, above all, a rhythm. It started about the turn of the twentieth century and has been evolving ever since. It can be sung to any tune, in any key, with any number of lines, to convey any mood. So many have been, and are being, created that they haven't decanted yet. For the last few decades there has been a creative avalanche—just as happened in earlier days with the fandango and before with that the soleá. So, except for its underlying rhythm, and the fact that it is festive, the best you can say is that *la bulería lo traga todo* (the bulería can swallow anything).

The twelve-count is the same as for the soleares and alegrías, that is, the twelve-count of

$$. \ . \ | \ . \ . \ | \ . \ | \ . \ | \ . \ |$$

but you won't get far if you try to measure it this way. The rhythms and counterrhythms are endlessly varied and complicated. To detail the palmas a bit: you will hear some people clapping all six beats, others marking 1 2 3 4 5 (6), still others marking 1 2 (3) 4 5 (6), and so on. In Jerez the count is in units of six beats, rather than the twelve of elsewhere, but either way it ends on a strong tenth beat:

1 2 3 4 5 6 / 1 2 3 4 (5 6).

The guitar is played in either position. You will hear from the recorded example that it supplies much of the syncopation, and its falsetas are an endless source of rhythmic and melodic invention.

The words may be anything: satirical, caustic, topical, sentimental—whatever mood the singer feels like conveying—and in any number of lines from three upward.

The Song Forms

No quiero na contigo	I don't want anything to do with you
te rebelas con mi mare	you rebel against my mother
eres mi mayor castigo.	you're my worst punishment.

Tirando piedras por las calles	I'm throwing stones out of the window
y a quien le dé que lo perdone	and if they hit anyone, I'm sorry.
Tengo mi cabecita loca	It's just that I'm going crazy
de puras cavilaciones.	from all this thinking.

When the famous Lole went on tour without her husband, I heard her sister sing:

Cantando, la Lola	Lole has gone singing
se va por las mares	overseas
y no critícala porque va sola:	don't accuse her for going alone:
se va con sus pesares.	she's taken her sadness for company.

Melchora Ortega put a verse about her little son in her prizewinning song:

Sereno, por Dios, sereno	For God's sake, nightwatchman
no pegue la voz tan alta	stop calling so loud,
que está mi Dani durmiendo	my Dani's asleep.

El Torta has never stinted on wine, women, or song. This bulería is one of his:

Ne ne ne ne ne	Ne ne ne ne ne
que me vengo cayendo	I'm stumbling along,
que de la borracherita	from a little booze-up,
del vino que tengo.	from the wine I've got aboard.
Esta noche voy a hablar ya	Tonight I'm going to talk to the moon
a la luna	

para decirle lo mucho que la quiero	tell her how much I love her
y de noche sueño con ella	how I dream of her at night
y hasta la acaricio el pelo	and even stroke her hair
y le diré	and I'll tell her
que tiene los dientes blancos	she has white teeth
y los acaes negros	and black eyes
y le diré	and I'll tell her
que tiene los labios tristes	she has lips as sad
como un atardecer que se va muriendo	as the dying of twilight
y que conozca que lleva mi pensamiento.	and I want her to know I'm thinking of her.

At the end of chapter 3 I mentioned Tomasito's rap bulerías. Here is an extract from one:

A mi puerta llamo una robotina marciana	A martian robotess knocked at my door
y en mi casita se metió	and settled in my house
robotín, robotán, robotín, robotán . . .	roboty robota roboty robota
tú comes tuercas y tornillos y no te pasa ná	you eat nuts and bolts, no problem,
y este torrotrón que es para bailar	and this torrotron is for dancing to
que estoy robotizao	I've been robotized
y no puedo parar.	and I can't stop.

No wonder the kids at the feria liked him.

The dance is crammed with vitality and always comic, perhaps even more so when not performed by professional dancers. Performances, whether on stage or in the clubs, tend to finish with what is called a *fin de fiesta*, which consists of bulerías sung by all the singers and danced by all, whoever they are—singers, dancers, guitarists, and palmeros. I have a photo that shows the dancers falling about at the comic dancing of the palmero Luis de La Tota. This dance, considered by outsiders the hardest of all, is within reach of all flamencos, however young. It brings us back to the fundamental principle of all *baile*: that flamencos have had the rhythms inside them since before they could walk and can dance these rhythms whether they are dancers or not.

A postscript on Andalusian gesture and dance: An Andalusian may express "Oh! no" by a hand flung up with a sinuous flick of the wrist; it is a dancer's movement, graceful and expressive. And so are many of the gestures of the Andalusians: they are spacious and either forceful or graceful, rather than merely conventional. Someone once remarked that it is no wonder they dance so well: they all walk like dancers—yes, but they *talk* like dancers too, with their hands and arms. Conversely, in the dance of the bulería (at least as done by Jerezanos, admitted specialists at it) you see everyday gestures *turned* into dance—adopted, parodied, and stylized. Some of these gestures would be quite unacceptable if not thus formalized. But being formalized in syncopated form, they are acceptable and can be wickedly funny. The nine-year-old on the far left in figure 1, already used to dancing in public, incorporates into his bulería gestures for which his mother would smack him if he made them around the house.

The performance on track 6 is by Melchora Ortega, winner of the Seville Bienal singing prize in 1998, accompanied by Pascual de Lorca. It was recorded in a peña, and you can hear the jaleo of the audience, which becomes vociferous when she breaks into dance at the end of each verse.

✦ Tangos, tientos, and tanguillos
   Track 7

The **tiento-tango** is probably the oldest flamenco song form in a simple rhythm familiar to all of us. It is in 2/4 time, as reflected in the rhythm beaten out by the palmeros. Variations exist, but mostly the form is a two-bar unit with a silence on the first beat, two claps on the second, and then a clap on each beat of the second bar, thus: **. ıı ıı**.

The guitar always plays *en medio* (as for A); and usually, as in track 7, the guitarist plays the notes B–G–A as a sort of leitmotif whenever the singer pauses, which he couldn't do if playing *por arriba.*

The tiento tune is often relatively easy for us non-flamencos to hear beneath the singer's flamenco melismas, though track 7 may not make this clear. It interests me particularly because of one phrase. The singer starts with a rise from E to A via G-sharp—this also happens in the soleá de Alcalá, though here it is much easier for Western ears because of the clear and lilting 2/4 rhythm—but in the tiento you sometimes hear the singer go back down to the E via the same G-sharp. This gives A–G-sharp–F–E. I have tried throughout to avoid musical jargon and I apologize to nonmusicians for this bit, but the fact is the interval between F-natural and G-sharp is rare outside Semitic music, whether Jewish or Arabic. I don't want to persuade anybody of anything, except perhaps the origins of flamenco in an ethnic mix. Above all, this interval sounds richly exotic.

The dance of the tiento, performed by women (I have never seen it performed by men), has a certain stately dignity. Not so the tango.

The words of the tiento may reflect various moods, more often than not on themes of love:

Si el mundo llama vivir	If the world calls living
a vivir como yo vivo	living the way I live
mil veces pido la muerte	then let's have death
porque para mi vivir	because living means having you
es tenir a ti, y a ti no tengo.	and I don't have you.

The words of the tango are more festive, as suits its pace, and often have an acerbic or satirical note:

Quítate de la esquina	Get away from my corner
chiquillo loco	crazy boy
que tu madre no te quiere	your mother doesn't love you
ni yo tampoco.	and nor do I.
Gitana mi madre	My mother is a Gypsy
gitana mi abuela	my grandmother too
y la madre de mis hijos	and the mother of my children
es canastera.	is a basket weaver.

(No trade is more typically Gypsy than that of basket weaver.)

In Franco's days, La Niña de los Peines sang:

Triana, que bonita está Triana	Triana, how pretty it is
cuando le ponen al puente	when its bridge is decorated
las banderitas gitanas.	with Gypsy banners.

There *are* no Gypsy banners. The flamencos all knew that the words were originally *banderas republicanas* (with Republican banners), and they loved her for it.

I recorded track 7 in a flamenco locale in Cádiz. It is sung by María del Mar Fernández, a young singer, who, I think, has a future: she has a powerful voice with a very flamenco timbre, and sang this one for me without microphone. The people of Cádiz (Gaditanos) are indeed different in their approach to flamenco. They have a reputation for festive songs but I hadn't realized to what point this influenced their performance until I recorded this track. When María del Mar sang a soleá and a fandango, it was almost as if she were paying her dues: the audience hardly reacted at all. The rest of the evening was all festive—tiento/tangos, alegrías, colombianas, bulerías—and these had the audience shouting their jaleo. For her *fin de fiesta*, she merely nodded to people in the audience, and the gesture produced a dervish performance of more than a dozen, singing and dancing like mad. Cádiz likes its flamenco with tunes and without pain.

María del Mar's song should make clear that the flamenco tango has nothing to do with the Argentine dance. When sung on its own, its tune differs from that of the tiento, though not its rhythm. The tune varies but is commonly characterized by a four-note sequence, starting high and falling down the scale. If you can, it will be easier to listen to this in Saura's film *Flamenco* (see appendix 2), where you will also hear a second part to the tune, which it shares with the tiento and is explained in my notes. Usually—that is, outside Cádiz—the tango is short and is merely sung as a way of ending the tiento, using the same tune speeded up. But here we are in Cádiz, where having fun is the priority. So she sings the tiento slower than usual, making it sound like a plaintive introduction to the festive tango, in which she uses various tunes and many verses (the original lasts over ten minutes).

The **tanguillos** are songs of Cádiz, where, to quote one tanguillo,

Reina una gracia tan fina	There is so much grace and wit
que hasta las gallinas	that even the hens
ponen huevos con sal.	lay their eggs with salt [lay witty eggs].

The songs are festive, light, sometimes mocking, always suitable for Carnival—which in Cádiz beats any other this side of Rio de Janeiro, since the Gaditanos are even better than other Andaluces at letting rip in celebration. Having said that, the tanguillo is *not* flamenco. It is in 2/4 time, in a major key, with a three-chord vamp to accompany it—never a trace of the flamenco mode or rhythms. The words tell a story, usually a tall one, or what used to be called a shaggy-dog story. It is easy to recognize: if you hear an upbeat song in tango rhythm, with a tune that seems perfectly familiar in style, and which goes on a bit, you can safely bet it is a tanguillo. The following example should make the point. It was sung by Chano Lobato, a fine singer and great entertainer.

A la venta ponen	The antique dealers
estos anticuarios	are putting on sale
esta gran cazuela que tiene	this fine, big stewpot
más de quinientos años.	more than five hundred years old.
La doy en mil duros	I'll sell it for five thousand
y es casi de balde	almost a giveaway price
y esta gran cazuela tenía	for this same stewpot you see here
un mérito bastante grande:	has had a remarkable history:
La cazuela que aquí les presento es	This pot that I'm offering is made of
de una sustancia que nadie conoce	a substance that nobody's heard of;
fabricada en Medina Sidonia	it was made in Medina Sidonia
el año cuarenta del siglo catorce.	in the year thirteen hundred and forty.
La tenía don Pedro Zorullo	It was owned by Don Pedro Zorullo
que era temporero de la catedral	the cathedral official who used it
se lavaba los pies los domingos	on Sundays for washing his feet in
y luego los lunes hacía espoleá.	and on Mondays for cooking his stew.

✦ Cantiñas: alegrías, caracoles, mirabrás, romeras, and rosas
Track 8

The cantiñas group includes the **alegrías**, and these are by far the most common. Until the bulerías began to take over, in the course of the twentieth century, it was the most popular of the festive song forms, which is natural for a song originating, as it does, in Cádiz. As I describe in chapter 2, the tune (in 3/4 time) is in the major and either stays there or drops at the end to a fla-menco cadence; the guitar accompaniment is a three-chord vamp, which is to say it has the same harmonies as "Happy Birthday to You." Even the pal-mas have the regularity of a pony trap trotting down the road. But—there is a big "but." As in all good flamenco, the performers—guitarist, singer, and dancer—transform these features. The guitarist dries out those vamp har-monies with discord; the singer's rhythmic subtleties cut across the trotting tempo; and, above all, the dancer creates a feast of subtle counter- and cross-rhythms.

The rhythm follows the same twelve-count as the soleá and the bulería—

.. I .. I . I . I . I

or

1 2 3 4 5 6 7 8 9 10 (11 12)

—but otherwise these three song forms have nothing at all in common. Above all, the alegrías started life as a song to dance to, and it remains a good dance (usually) for men. It is dominated by zapateado and tends to become a display of counterrhythms. Nevertheless, when sung without dance there is a world of difference between a routine rendering and a really good one. I wish I could put a finger on this difference, but I can't. The most I can say is that when well done, there is nothing commonplace about it. A good singer could make "God Save the Queen" sound flamenco.

The words traditionally tell of the charm of Cádiz or one of its inhabi-tants, though I recently heard Mijita Carpio sing one about his child.

The alegrías on track 8 are by Chano Lobato, a great entertainer as well as a master of the lighter forms of flamenco. He is accompanied on this example of alegrías by the guitarist Luis Moneo, who has himself recently become a fine singer. Here are Chano Lobato's words:

De que tu pases y no me hables	You passed me without speaking
qué cuidadito se me daba chiquilla a mí	and that upset me, girl,
¡ay! que yo no como ni bebo	I can't eat or drink
con buenos días de naide.	when people ignore me.
Tiré un tiro en el agua	I threw a stone in the sea
cayó en la arena	but it fell on the beach
confianza contigo,	no one can have
niña, no hay quien la tenga,	any trust in you, girl.
El sentío me da vueltas	My head spins round
compañerita de mi alma	girlfriend of my soul
(de mis entrañas)	(body and soul)
y yo me arrimo a las paredes	I have to lean on the walls
hasta llegar a tu puerta	until I reach your door.
Como tú eres bonita mucho presumes	Being so pretty
que te vas a poner más alta	you set yourself higher
que van las nubes	than the clouds
que van las nubes.	than the clouds.

The recording is taken from the album *De Jerez a los puertos* by kind permission of Manuel Morao and Gitanos de Jerez S.L.

The other forms of cantiña are less commonly heard. They all have the same or similar guitar accompaniment, but with different tunes, and with words on different themes. The alegrías has three parts to its tune, the third part or *macho* going up higher before tumbling down to the end. The other cantiñas also date from the nineteenth century; many of them derive from songs from the popular Spanish form of operetta, the zarzuela.

The **caracoles** started in a zarzuela as a street snail-vendor's song. It has Madrid associations, including the verse

113

Como reluce	How splendid is
la gran calle de Alcalá	Alcalá Street
cuando suben y bajan	when the Andalusians
los Andaluces.	stroll up and down it.

The original verse in the operetta was

"No son tan chicos."	"They're not small enough."
¡Caramba!	Heck!
"Venga otro cuarto."	"Give me another quarter."
¡Hermosa!	You're pretty!
"No los quiero."	"Don't want them."
Usté es faisiosa	You're fussy
y yo soy muy liberal.	And I'm very liberal.

The last word is a covert political declaration. Spain's history over the last two centuries has been one of attempts at liberalism (they invented the word), followed by reactionary backlash.

The **mirabrás** uses that word (which has no meaning that I can discover) in its refrain. It may date from the Napoleonic wars, since its usual words have a flavor reminiscent of the Liberal Declaration of 1811:

A mí qué me importa	What do I care
que un rey me culpe,	that the king indites me,
si el pueblo es grande y me abona?	if the people are great and back me?
Voz del pueblo, voz del cielo.	Voice of the people, voice of God.

Cádiz was the only city never to fall to the French. The declaration was made there and inspired the South American countries to break away from Spain.

The **romera** sings of a girl on pilgrimage. The word *romería* applies to any from the great pilgrimage to Santiago, or to the Virgin of the Dew in marshlands of the Coto Doñana, down to a village outing, such as one I described a few years ago in my book on Andalusia:

> There was a village *romería* going on. This may occasionally involve thousands of people, with colour and music and display. But for a forgotten village like Belerda it is a cross between a holiday, a pilgrimage, a picnic and a country walk. There were a priest, a couple of nuns and upwards of a hundred villagers, nearly all young, the small boys lagging behind to throw stones or fight, the girls in giggling gaggles, or singing arm in arm and, somewhere in the middle, a group of them taking turns to carry the Virgin. When they got to whichever little country shrine they were heading for, they would have their picnic, say a few Aves and Novenas, laugh a bit, play a bit, sing a few hymns and as many other songs as they could drum up. I expect their folksongs would be interspersed with Paul McCartney and Paul Simon; but all, whether hymns or pop, would be sung in those slightly shrill voices harmonized at a third throughout, and with an added touch of Andalusian turns and quarter-tones in the cadences.

The **rosa** is still rarer and, for its words, even harder to distinguish. Anything else will be called a cantiña and named after its place of origin, or else the singer who first made it, or after a popular song of the nineteenth century. Its tune differs mainly in that at the end the voice stays up, rather than coming down to the tonic.

To sum up: all have tunes that are more Western folk song than flamenco; all are cantiñas; if they go a bit faster and praise Cádiz, they are alegrías; if they sing of a girl in the country, they are likely to be romeras; if they sing of Madrid and Alcalá Street, they will be caracoles; and if they use the word "mirabrás," they are mirabrás; otherwise they are called cantiñas.

Chapter 5

✦ Polo and caña

You will occasionally hear the polo and caña—especially performed for dancers. But they are in some way vestiges of flamenco prehistory, and somewhat ossified. They are certainly old: the **polo** is mentioned in the eighteenth century, and the **caña** early in the nineteenth. Indeed, they seem to invite historical comment. De Falla was the leading light in organizing a competition for pure *cante jondo* in 1922. It was won by Tenazas ("The Pliers") with a caña he had learned from Silverio, a pivotal figure of nineteenth-century song, who had himself probably learned it from El Fillo, one of the earliest known singers. So Tenazas's words probably go back two hundred years:

En el querer no hay venganza	Love has no place for vengeance
y tú te has vengado de mí	and you took revenge on me
castigo tarde o temprano	heaven, sooner or later,
del cielo te ha de venir.	will send you your punishment.

Singers find the forms constricting, so that it is not surprising that today, when they are mostly sung for dancers, the caña and the polo have lost the force they had for Tenazas.

The experts underline the differences between between the polo and the caña, but for our purposes they are minimal. Their common features dominate: both are sung to a rigid form consisting of a four-line verse with *ay!* repeated in a sequence, sounding rather as a refrain, after the second and fourth lines. Both have the soleá compás and are accompanied as a soleá. Both used to be sung rather fast (so, as a soleá por bulería) but today tend to be sung with the *ayes* very slow. The tunes of both, while not identical, cover a whole octave, coming down the scale in stages from E to C to A (or G) and then from C again down to the flamenco final E. There are differences in the tune of the *ayes*: in the caña, they are sung within a range of three notes from the flamenco E; in the polo they rise a bit higher. But even here, singers often mix them up.

The songs are often rounded off with a verse from another song form, pitched higher—the polo with a bit of soleá; the caña with the same or a polo.

The words are usually as archaic as those of Tenazas. I notice that a recent CD (1999) that concentrates on the polo and caña as dance forms, and was made by up-and-coming performers, uses only very old words (one of them from a fifteenth-century ballad).

Carmona tiene una fuente	There's a fountain in Carmona
con catorce o quince caños	with fourteen or fifteen spouts
con un letrero que dice	and an inscription that reads
Viva el polo de Tobalo.	Hurrah for Tobalo's polo.
Tu eres el diablo, romera,	You are the devil, pilgrim girl,
que me vienes a tentar	who has come to tempt me.
No soy el diablo, romera,	I'm no devil, pilgrim girl,
que soy tu mujer natural.	I am your wedded wife.

✦ **Peteneras**
Track 9

Legendary or real, La Petenera was a girl from Paterna de la Rivera (Cádiz), notorious for her beauty and hardness of heart. A nineteenth-century writer mentions hearing **peteneras** sung in a voice that conveyed "inexplicable sadness." The song still does. Flamencoization has left it strangely untransformed. Despite the melismas, quarter tones, and rubato any flamenco singer adds, its haunting tune remains recognizable. What is more, unlike most other flamenco music, it can be written down. So can its time signature: a bar of 6/8 followed by one of 3/4.

Chapter 5

It is not commonly danced, in spite of having a regular time signature. And when it is danced, only the "short" version is used (the tunes differ slightly), and the only rhythm added is that of finger-snapping by the dancer herself, who usually wears a shawl on her head, perhaps as a reference to its Jewish associations. The short and long versions do not differ greatly: you can hear a verse of each in the recording. The guitarist plays *por arriba*. His falsetas, both in the introduction and between verses, use and repeat the melody of the song, and the tune leans toward the minor. Contrast this with the soleá or the tiento, in which the guitar falsetas have their own themes.

The Gypsies have the same superstition about the petenera as British actors have about *Macbeth*: they perform it, but the title must never be named. I bumped into this in the Sacromonte cave known as the Zambra de María la Canastera. Her grandson was recording palo rhythms for me, under the eye of his father, when I asked for peteneras. Consternation—as much the young and emancipated son's as his traditionally minded father's.

The petenera has Jewish associations. The Israeli musicologist Susana Weich-Shahak tells me the tune is still sung, to other words, among the Sephardim of the Middle East. The words certainly have strong Jewish echoes. When it was folk song, before being flamencoized, it may have helped them as an outlet for their feelings. It must be remembered that the Jewish population of Spain had been considerable since Old Testament days: the prophet Obadiah mentions the "servants of the Lord that are in Sepharad" (Spain and Portugal), and Jonah was heading that way when he got swallowed by his whale. In 1492 Queen Isabella ordered them to abjure their faith and convert to Christianity or else leave the country. That agonizing dilemma affected at least 200,000 people who had lived there for upward of a thousand years. Those who could not bear to leave first had to forswear their own God and then found that the Inquisition was set on them. In private they could use the petenera to express their true feelings. At least this would account for the Jewish references in the text of the various versions. In the first two stanzas that follow, the word *renegar* (renounce, abjure, deny) is a heavily charged one. To abjure the God you believe in must have been a traumatic experience.

Quisiera yo renegar
de este mundo por entero
volver de nuevo a habitar,
¡mare de mi corazón!
por ver si en un mundo nuevo
encontraba más verdad.

I would like to abjure everything,
renounce this whole world
and come back and live again,
mother of my heart!
to see if in a new world
I could find any more truth.

Y reniega por su suerte
porque se muere de sed.
Soy como el que va a la fuente
¡mare de mi corazón!
y se encuentra que está seca
y, al no poderla beber
humildemente se aleja.

And his fate is to abjure
because he is dying of thirst.
I am like one who goes to the well
mother of my heart!
and finds it dry
and, being unable to drink,
walks humbly away.

Al pie de un pocito seco
de rodillas me hinqué
fueron tan grandes los llantos
que el pocito rebosé.

By the side of a dry well
I went down on my knees
and wept so hard
that I filled the well.

By the waters of Babylon . . . ? In the light of words such as these I find nothing "inexplicable" in the sadness heard in this song. They are heartbreaking.

The words more commonly sung today tell of the hardhearted beauty La Petenera:

Quien te puso Petenera
no supo ponerte nombre
te debía de poner
madre de mi corazón
te debía de poner
la perdición de los hombres.

Whoever called you Petenera
got your name wrong
he should have called you
mother of my heart
he should have called you
damnation of men.

Si oyes doblar las campanas
no preguntes quien ha muerto
porque a ti te lo dirá
tu mismo remordimiento.

If you hear the bell toll
don't ask who has died
your own remorse
will tell you.

You may hear one or two verses that don't quite fit either theme but that suggest a vague folk memory that this song once concerned the persecuted Jews:

¿Adónde vas, bella judía,
tan compuesta y a deshora?
Voy en busca de Rebeco
que está en la sinagoga.

Beautiful Jewess, where are you going
so calm and at such a late hour?
I'm going in search of Rebeco
who is in the synagogue.

Presumably Rebeco is a vague memory of the name Rebecca. The final example mixes both themes. It concerns the cruel Petenera, but there is one spine-chilling detail: within Spain a "missionary of God" could only have been an Inquisitor.

Tú, misionero de Diós
si la encuentras por ahí
dile que yo me contento
con que se acuerda de mí
en cada día un momento.

Oh you, missionary of God,
if you meet her somewhere
tell her I am content
for her to remember me
for one moment in each day.

If the missionary did meet up with her, she would be unable to think of me, even for a moment: she would only think of the pain.

The performance on track 9 is by Juan Zarzuela, with guitar by Pedro Pimentel. Both are young and promising, though Juan has been singing in public since he was twelve and has the maturity to sing this with appropriate simplicity, while the guitarist's youth shows in his opening falsetas, which are in a style perhaps more fashionable than one suited to the character of the song.

♦ The fandango family: verdiales, fandangos locales, fandangos de Huelva, rondeñas, malagueñas, jaberas, fandangos personales or fandangos grandes, and granaínas
   Tracks 10–15

The **fandango** is thought to be Moorish in origin. It spread through Spain and then Europe and was immensely popular in the eighteenth century— Mozart had to include one in *The Marriage of Figaro*, since his opera is set in Spain. Some people say it then came back to Andalusia and became a flamenco song form, but in fact it never left the hinterland of Málaga, where the verdiales are still traceably Moorish. The fandangos are a vast family that includes all the *cantes de levante*, which I have put into the next section. It goes all the way from the easily accessible folk verdiales to the fandango grande (or fandango personal), which is in free rhythm and is the one that sounds most weird and unmusical to non-flamenco ears. Every province has its own versions of it; in the city of Granada there are at least three; and the province of Huelva has a dozen or more.

The fandango's basic form, in strict rhythm, is easy to recognize: the time signature is 3/4, and the rhythm is that of Ravel's *Bolero*. It has six musical phrases, although the verse has only five lines, of which one is repeated, whole or in part; and the harmonic structure given to it by the guitar is that the phrases end on the major chords on C, F, C, G, C, F–E. You will remember from chapter 4 that this slide from F to E is the equivalent of the "perfect" cadence (from G to C) of Western music: in each case it makes the listener feel that the song is complete, that we have come to the end. There are occasional variations on this scheme, which I mention where relevant.

(A parenthesis for musicians here. It may be worth noting that this somewhat commonplace harmonic sequence is only schematic. A competent flamenco guitarist will enrich it, not only by his improvisations, but, as it were, by drying the chords out with discordant notes. I notice, for example, that the Cordoban guitarist Merengue, even when playing the folksy and basic fandangos de Huelva, where the cadence is a sequence of major triads on G, F, and E, leaves an E in his chord of G major and builds the so-called F chord on F, C, F, G, B, and E—however you would name that.)

Whether they are in strict rhythm (verdiales, locales, rondeñas, and those from Huelva) or in free rhythm (personal fandangos, malagueñas, jaberas, and granaínas), all fandangos have words in five-line stanzas with the scheme of rhyme (or assonance) *ababa*. If you are not familiar with assonance (which, in Spanish, is commoner than rhyme), it occurs in the original (British) version of "Pop Goes the Weasel."

> Half a pound of tupenny rice
> Half a pound of *treacle*
> That's the way the money goes
> Pop goes the *weasel*.
> Up and down the City Road
> In and out the *Eagle*
> That's the way the money goes
> Pop goes the *weasel*.

Verdiales are a folk dance from the hill villages behind Málaga, and I put them first in the fandango family because to move from this form through others is to move from a simple folk dance in fixed and emphatic rhythm through the whole flamencoizing process. Unlike the fandangos of Huelva, which are also folk music, verdiales tend to be sung solo, but the accompaniment may be a whole band consisting of guitars, *bandurrias*, fiddle, drum, and tambourines. The bandurria is a metal stringed instrument, rather like a flat-backed mandolin. If you cross the straits to the Mahgreb (which is only the Arabic word for the West, but is a convenient way of referring to the countries from Tunisia to Morocco), you will find music made by the same instruments. The style of the verdiales sets the pattern for all the folk fandangos or fandangos locales, except those of Huelva.

I use a **fandango local** to illustrate what I have described above. The words mostly sing the praises of the village, its patron saint, its wine, or the singer's girlfriend.

Of the verses below, one is from the province of Almería; the other is a self-mocking one from Facinas, a village in Cádiz province.

Viva el reino de Almería	Long live the kingdom of Almeria
donde nacen los tempranos	where the grapes grow early
viva el reino de Almería,	long live the kingdom of Almeria,
tierra de los minerales,	land of minerals,
mujeres guapas y bravías	where the women are wild and pretty
y de los hombres cabales.	and the men are the best.
En el año de la pera	In the year when the pears were good,
dijeron los de Facinas	the Facinas folk said
a los de la Ventolera,	to the folk from Ventolera,
en el año de la pera:	(in the year when the pears were good):
las mejores tagarninas	"We've got the best thistles
son las de nuestra ladera.	growing on our side of the hill."

123

Chapter 5

My example, on track 10, of the fandango local is the *Fandango of Frasquito Yerbagüena* from the Albaicín. The singer is Elisa La del Horno, and the guitarist is Rafael Hoces. For a fandango local it seemed appropriate to choose locals rather than professionals. My singer is a sweet old lady of seventy who sings like a girl, perhaps because she never had a childhood: her father was executed by the Falange (Fascist party) when she was small, and she had to leave school to help her mother survive. I discovered this when I asked her for the words: she hesitated, then said would I mind if she spelled them wrong? So I told her I had learned my Spanish working in France for those who had managed to escape over the Pyrenees. Her eyes lit up at the thought of that. I *like* this performance.

The words, in this case, show devotion to the Virgin Mary, patron of Granada, though her last verse is more typical of the fandango local:

Quiero vivir en Granada	I want to live in Granada
porque me gusta el oír	because I like to hear
la campana de la Vela	the watchtower bell
cuando me voy a dormir	while I'm going to sleep.

(The watchtower and its bell are on the castle of the Alhambra.)

The province of Huelva has little flamenco but, in contrast, umpteen folk fandangos (**fandangos de Huelva**) that were taken up by flamenco singers not long ago and have become popular. Most villages seem to have their own. They differ slightly in rhythm from the verdiales model by the use of triplets, and more notably in the tunes. As is the case with all fandangos, all the tunes start and finish in the E mode, but instead of climbing into C major they often move into A minor or else swerve into A major and stay there until the final F–E cadence.

The songs are usually cheerful and upbeat, with themes similar to those I quote for other local fandangos. The rhythmic, harmonic, and melodic variations also extend to the verse form, which occasionally has a four-line refrain. The following example is sung so cheerfully that the intent is clearly mockery of the great lover who tries it on with all the girls.

Dime si te llamas Cinta	Tell me: is your name Jacinta?
o te llamas Concepción	or are you possibly Conchita?
o si te llamas Rocío	or am I talking to Rocío?
morena de mi pasión.	O black-haired girl whom I adore.

The **rondeña** is so called because it comes from Ronda, of which Richard Ford said in 1840 that to see it was alone worth the voyage out and back again—quite a recommendation, considering he had to sail across the Bay of Biscay in a packet-boat and ride some fifty miles from Cádiz up through the hills. Some flamencologists claim the word means a serenade to be sung during the nighttime round (*ronda*) of the streets—which is presumably the same as what young Frenchmen, mixing their metaphors, call "trawling for kittens." "Facts" about flamenco usually turn out to be no more than somebody's theory—but then mere theory becomes fact when singers believe these experts and make their verses accordingly. So now the rondeña *is* often a serenade.

It is a fandango of two verses, sung in strict tempo though not usually danced. Spanish speakers may notice that the verse is a strictly rhyming *quintilla* (in Andalusian Spanish *Diós* does rhyme with *amor*, and *besé* with *dejé*). There are two tunes, though the first one you hear on track 13 is the more common and is often sung alone. I chose this version as a good example of a fandango in rhythm, which is clearly flamenco rather than folk. You can hear it in the singer's pushing and pulling on the beat, as well as his play with pitch. The performance is by Juan Zarzuela, with Pedro Pimentel on guitar.

Anda y no digas, por Diós,	Get away, don't try to tell me
que me quieres más que a nadie	that you love me more than anyone;
anda y no digas, por Diós,	get away, don't try to tell me.
que las palabras de amor	For words of love
las va deshojando el aire	are blown away by the wind
como deshoja la flor.	as petals are blown off the flower.

Te conocí en la Alcazaba	I met you in the Alcazaba
y en el Palo te besé;	on the Palo I kissed you;
y en la Caleta llorabas	and on the Caleta you wept,
el día que te dejé	the day I left you for another
por otra que me esperaba.	who was waiting for me.

The **malagueña** is characterized by its sad, elegiac tone. The city and province of Málaga are virtually the home of the flamenco fandango. Except for the folk fandangos of Huelva, many of them seem to have originated here and spread outward—west to Ronda, north to Lucena, and, above all, north and east throughout Granada, Jaen, and Almería. In Málaga province you find the early, almost Moorish folk verdiales and the serenadelike fandangos of Ronda, but in Málaga itself the malagueña becomes more flamencoized, that is, more personal, slower, and freer of rhythm. It sticks rigidly to the fandango structure of six musical phrases, which end, respectively, C, F, C, G, C, and F–E, but the free rhythm gives the singer more scope. This, in turn, means that the guitarist has to follow the singer and come in with the right harmonies at the right moments—an admirable skill, when you realize that they may never have met, or only long enough to agree on pitch.

The words are always sad and sometimes, as in the case of La Trini's, which I quote below, heartbreaking.

Alguna vez	Sometime
siquiera por compasión	if only out of pity

escríbeme alguna vez	write to me sometime
que yo tengo el corazón	for my heart
marchito de padecer	is so withered with suffering
que ya no siente ni el dolor.	that it can no longer even feel the pain.

The tunes vary but stay within the harmonic framework mentioned above. But the guitar (always played *por arriba*), though it commonly starts with a long rasgueado on E moving to F, always tends toward a tuneful fili-gree of runs and tremolos. It gives the singer his entry by a phrase based on the harmonic sequence A minor–G major–F major–E major, though this may be disguised by the embroidery, and it almost always ends with an arpeggio up the E major chord. You are unlikely to hear it ended as in my example with a fast fandango verdial, yet this is a traditional way of doing it and might help you by relating the malagueña in its free rhythm to the fan-dango in the rhythm from which it stemmed.

Unlike the other fandangos in free rhythm, such as the granaína and the personal fandango, the malagueña has only one verse: if you hear two, they are two malagueñas. It is always in the five-line *quintilla* form with the rhyme (or assonance) scheme *ababa*.

I mentioned earlier in the section on the malagueña that the guitarist has to follow the singer, and since in some instances they will never have met before, this requires much skill. This is not the case, though, in the malagueña heard on track 12, a performance by Dolores Agujeta accompa-nied by her son Antonio, known as Agujetas Chico. I take it from a promo-tional disk, *Dolores Agujeta, hija del duende*, with their kind permission.

The **jaberas** are a form of fandango from Málaga, not often sung—and, since they are in free rhythm, not danced. The name is said to refer to a bean seller (who might be called an *habera*)—another speculation as debatable as any, since nobody seems to have known anyone in such a specialist trade. The nature of the song itself makes me lean toward the idea that it came from fishermen who go to sea in the local boats called *jabegas*. (This is not as far-fetched as it might seem, for the Andalusian way of speech makes *jabera* and *jabega* virtually indistinguishable.) The song has long-held high notes and a simple melodic line that runs up and down the scale, so it would ring out over a calm sea with an exuberance that would suit open spaces far better than enclosed ones (other, perhaps, than your bathroom). It also has florid vocal decoration, which the singer adds only to the downward scale. He then runs straight up again in rapid eighth notes, so that the song makes me think of someone running up a slope in order to turn cartwheels down it. It differs from other fandangos in that the guitar simply alternates between C major and G major chords until the final descent to the Andalusian cadence of F–E. Indeed, it has occurred to me, on the few occasions I have heard it, that it would sound better unaccompanied—as would be the case on a fishing boat.

Of all the fandangos in free rhythm, the **fandango personal** or **fandango grande** is the freest, the hardest to characterize—and the one most often sung. It is immensely and abidingly popular wherever flamencos gather, whatever the province. This is because, in a way, it is the most flamenco of song forms in that the tune is nothing, while the words, together with the emotional and powerful expression of them, are everything. It keeps to the musical form of six phrases ending respectively on the major chords C, F, C, G, C, and F–E, and it is passionate. But it is not characterized by any single mood, such as the sadness of the malagueña or the ecstatic lyricism of the granaína. It may have any number of verses, and it would not help to quote a tune, since there are so many. The guitar (usually played *por arriba*) has no specific phrase acting as a "signature," either for the singer's entry or to finish the piece.

The fandango grande is the song form that, perhaps, gives most importance to the melismas, and the singer's bravura display of them at the end gives musical point to the words and rouses the enthusiasm of the audience. So the words are especially important. I give several examples, some of them old ones; each comes to a dramatic climax on the last line that gives artistic point to the melismatic outburst at the end. We have such a strong tradition of cultured, literary verse that we easily lose the capacity to appreciate the qualities of oral poetry. Yet here you see lyrics in the original sense of the word: lines composed to be sung. There are many hundreds of them, and they are still often composed by the singer.

This first one probably dates from the Spanish-American War at the end of the nineteenth century:

A mi me podrán llamar	They can call me to arms
a servir a Dios y al rey	to serve God and my king,
pero apartarme de ti	but no law orders me
no me lo manda la ley	to part from you;
mejor consiento morir.	I'd rather die.

This one is also from the bad old days:

Y una ronda me alcanzaba,	A patrol had nearly caught me;
mi jaca, de muerte hería,	my mare was badly wounded;
por salvarme galopaba.	she galloped to save me.
Murió salvando mi vía,	She died saving my life,
y por la bella lloraba.	and I wept for her, the beauty.

The third is El Torre's, whose singing affected his audiences as powerfully as John Wesley's preaching—people wept and ripped their shirts:

Blanca paloma te traigo	I brought you a white dove
que del nío la cogí.	that I took from the nest.
La madre se queó llorando	Its mother was left weeping,
como yo lloré por ti.	as I have wept for you.
La solté y salió volando.	So I let it go and it flew away.

129

In this next one, the melismatic outburst on the last line would feel familiar to any tenor who has sung in Bach's *St. Matthew Passion* "and he went out and wept bitterly."

De que no había mujer buena iba diciendo ayer tarde	I was saying yesterday that there was no such thing as a good woman.
volví la cara pa' atrás y me encontré con mi mare: de pena me eché a llorar.	I looked behind me and found my mother there: I wept for sorrow.
Si lo vendes por dinero ponle precio a tu querer que si vale el mundo entero pa comprarlo robaré y que Diós me ampare luego.	If you sell it for money set a price on your love: if you ask the whole world I'll steal to buy it, and may God protect me after.
Yo a dormir me acostaba porque olvidarte yo quería. Cuanto más durmiendo estaba más presente te tenía porque contigo soñaba.	I lay down to sleep to try to forget you. The deeper I slept the more you stayed with me, because you were in my dream.
Yo entré un día en el manicomio me pesó haberlo hecho; yo vi una loca en el patio, se sacaba y daba el pecho a una muñeca de trapo	One day I went to the asylum; I regretted doing so: in the yard I saw a madwoman giving her breast to suckle a rag doll.

The dancer María Bermúdez (known in the United States as "Chacha") tells me that the words often hide a second meaning, making their pull that

much the stronger among those who know. But this is an introduction to flamenco, and such meanings would be beyond the reach of such as you and
me. I mention it only as an extra dimension of the skill and art of oral poetry.

Track 11, a recording of a fandango personal, gives you a taste of spontaneous flamenco sung without guitar (*a palo seco*). I recorded it in my apartment when a flamenco came round to call.

The **granaína** is a form of fandango in free rhythm that in many ways
stands apart. The Alhambra is not the only sign of the Moors' influence in
Granada. Among many other things, their richly ornamented poetry and
music should remind us that we got the word *arabesque* from these people.
Into his accompaniment to the granaína, the guitarist weaves sweet and
beautiful tremolo tunes; small wonder that the composer Tárrega chose to
call his famous tremolo study *Recuerdos de la Alhambra*. Granada is noted
both for its guitar makers and for the lyrical style of its guitar playing. So
much does the guitar accompaniment influence the mood of this song that,
in this one song form, the guitar seems to me as important as the singer—a
heresy worthy of the stake.

A few technical details for the musician/guitarist. The granaína is the
only song form in the key of B that is played on open strings—that is to say,
whether or not the guitar pitch is changed by use of the capodaster. What is
more, the chordal sequence is not quite the same as with other fandangos:
E minor/G–C–G–D7–G–C/B7. Thus the tonic B chord, even at the end, is
played with the flattened seventh, A. This makes it sound strangely incom-
plete and at the same time gives it a sort of yearning sweetness that accords
well with those moonlit tremolos. The singer's entry is always signaled by the
guitarist with a slide up the bass string from F-sharp to B, followed by the
plucking of the note B on both the open second string and the stopped
D string. Dryly technical as this may read, it is a further example of the
Granadan style of play, for it exploits the guitar's full resonance and makes
it sing out richly.

Figure 22. The dancer María Bermúdez ("Chacha"), a Californian.
Courtesy of the artist

Figure 23. Juan Antonio Tejero tours as a soloist with Chacha.
Courtesy of the artist

But perhaps what makes the granaína most stand apart is that it illustrates a curious phenomenon: the songs from the mountain areas tend to range wider over the gamut than those of the lowlands. It is as though the up-and-down of the mountains makes the songs and their accompaniment also range further up and down. A weird one for the ethnopsychologist (or psychoethnologist?) to consider. If such a wonderful beast exists.

The granaína is sung in two verses. Technically they are two songs; the first verse is sung to one, and in the second, the singer has to let rip with melismas over a wider range, a demanding test of vocal control. In their hometown they are called the half-granaína and granaína, but elsewhere are still misnamed the other way round. Though the half-granaína is bigger, its creator so named it out of respect for the granaína's creator. The words usually reflect the Granadino's passionate devotion to his city, an almost fanatic love expressed in poetry by the Moors in the Middle Ages, then in their laments when they were dispossessed, and then by the Christian conquerors who replaced them. I have chosen the traditional words sung by El Colorao, a Gypsy from the Albaicín, the old Moorish quarter of Granada.

Tu tienes una cruz al cuello	From your neck hangs a cross
engarzado en oro y marfil.	set in gold and ivory.
Déjame que muera en ella	Let me die on it
y crucificarme allí	and crucify myself there
en esa cruz que al cuello llevas.	on that cross that hangs from your neck.
Viva Graná la sultana	Long live Granada, the Moorish queen,
tierra que baña el Genil	land bathed by the river Genil.
Bendita sea la mañana	Blessed be the morning
en que yo te conocí	that I met you
con tu cara tan gitana.	with your pure Gypsy face.

In the recordings of the granaína on tracks 14 and 15, I use the two parts to show different sorts of performance—differences of occasion, style, and experience. Track 14 was recorded at a small-town provincial competition, with families sitting round tables with their cheese, serrano ham, and drink, babies being nursed, children hushed, and the murmured approval of the old man I was sharing a bottle with. The singer's performance is competent, but lackluster—she didn't reach the area final. Her accompanist, by contrast, is a star and perfectly illustrates the Granadan style. Track 15, the second part, is performed by a fine singer, whose stature and authority show in his climactic melismas and in the impact they make on his audience. They are a model of the art in their control and shaping: starting quietly, they build gradually both in range and in force. His command of the form also shows in the tempo, now fast, now lingering. To outsiders, the melismas often sound like a wild and tuneless wailing that hide the tune, as a mess of brambles might hide a garden statue. I can think of no singer more likely than El Colorao to persuade you otherwise, or at least to enable you to understand how an Andalusian musician can refer to "those delicious melismas that so enchant us."

But the differences in the two performances are above all between the non-Gypsy and Gypsy styles. The Gypsy singer of the second part puts more extreme energy and drama into his singing, while El Coquillo's tremolos do not attempt the lyrical beauty of the other guitarist's: being a Gypsy, he prefers rhythmic bite, punch, *pellizco*.

The girl singing in the first part of the recording uses traditional words whose theme dates back to the Middle Ages. Whether in song or ballad, it has always puzzled me that anyone should want to sleep under a rose bush, even if the rose is a metaphor. All those thorns!

Rosa, si yo no te cogí	Rose, I did not pluck you
fue porque no me dio ganas	for I did not want to do so.
al pie de un rosal dormí	I slept under a rose bower
y rosa tuve por cama	and a rose was my bed
y de cabecera, un jazmín.	and a jasmine my pillow.

✦ Cantes de Levante: tarantas, tarantos, mineras, cartageneras, and others
Tracks 16 and 17

All of the cantes de levante (songs of the east) are versions of a free-rhythm fandango that developed in the provinces of Almería, Jaen, and Murcia. The differences between them are so subtle that singers themselves often muddle them. Many simply announce they will sing a cante de levante and leave it at that. One point all these songs have in common is that the guitar always plays in the key of F-sharp, on open strings (or its equivalent if a capodaster is used to raise the pitch). In this key the guitarist has some strange discords that make the form immediately recognizable and add to the bitter, dark intensity of the taranta. For example, he plays the F-sharp major chord with an open B string and an open E string. The songs have another common characteristic in their use of a note that does not normally belong in the Andalusian mode or scale, but that does come into the guitarist's accompaniment to the fandango as a B-flat (described in chapter 4). In these eastern songs, the singer emphasizes it, makes it a key part of the melody.

The **taranta** is a mining song in free rhythm and by far the hardest to sing, demanding tragic intensity as well as unusual control, both vocal and artistic, in the melismas. In fact, few singers do it well. Among them, and one of the best alive, is Carmen Linares, whom you can hear singing it in Saura's *Flamenco*, which is easily obtainable on video. Her professional name shows why: the mining town of Linares is virtually the home of the taranta. I have chosen, instead, to illustrate the taranta with a solo guitar performance. It is a personal recording made, for this book, with his approval, of Juan Cortés "El Coquillo," who has since died of cancer. R.I.P.

Most guitar solos are not so much variations on the theme as the player's personal reactions to the music. This one was played by him in the early hours and gripped everyone. As we walked homeward in the gray dawn, I said I wished I could have recorded it. He paused, then said: "It wouldn't be the same," meaning that he had felt the duende. Later, he did let me record it, and though his performance wasn't as powerful, it still conveys some of the dark bleakness of the song.

The words of the taranta have only one theme: the hard life of the miner. This fact alone shows that flamenco does not belong exclusively to the Gypsies, since no Gypsy, now or ever, would choose the sunless daily grind of the miner's life. They had been enslaved in the mines in earlier days, the last instance being in the quicksilver mines of the central plateau in the 1740s, but the taranta was formed among the miners of eastern Andalusia in the mid-nineteenth century.

No se espante usté, señora
que es un minero el que canta:
con el humo de la mina,
tengo ronca la garganta.

Don't be frightened, lady,
it's a miner singing:
it's the dust from the mine
makes me sound so rough.

Bajo la mina pensando
si yo volveré a subir,
mientras bajo voy rezando
y cuando vuelvo a salir
me paso el tiempo cantando.

I go down the mine wondering
if I'll get out alive;
as I go down, I pray,
and when I do come up again
I spend my time singing.

Los mineros son leones
que los bajan enjaulados,
trabajan entre peñones
y allí mueren sepultados
dándole al rico millones.

Miners must be lions
since they're sent down in cages;
they work among the rock
and they die and are buried by it
to give the rich man millions.

The **taranto** is best explained as a danceable form of the taranta. It uses the same strange F-sharp accompaniment and is recognizably similar in tune and harmony to the taranta. Yet they are sung not only in rhythm, but in the 2/4 meter of the zambra (the same as the tango), which takes them fundamentally away from the 3/4 rhythms of the fandango from which these songs developed. And no less far from the lighthearted mood of the zambra, too. The words may express any theme, but they always have five lines, expanded or repeated to fit the fandango's six musical phrases. To my mind they make one of the better dances, an opinion confirmed by the María Bermúdez, who tells me she finds them hard because they demand so much intensity, but good to dance.

I choose to quote words by Manuel Torre, which are commonly heard.

¡Ay! mi muchacho	Oh! My son!
que hay tres días que no lo veo	I haven't seen him for three days
¡Ay! ¿dónde estará mi muchacho?	Oh! where can my son be?
Si estará bebiendo vino	He must have been drinking wine
y andará por ahí borracho	and wandering about drunk
¡Ay! alguna gitana me lo hará	Oh! some Gypsy girl will have got him.
entretenido.	

The performance of the taranto on track 17 is by Juan Pinilla, with the guitarist Carlos Zárate. Juan does use words about the mines.

Mineras are best described as watered-down tarantas. Indeed, they may have originated with singers who didn't have the vocal power or intensity to cope with a taranta. Except in this matter of intensity, they are pretty well indistinguishable from the taranta—not least among professional singers, and especially those who do not come from eastern Andalusia.

The **cartageneras** are derived from the taranta, though they are much closer to a malagueña in the guitarist's treatment of them. They have a florid vocal line, more "artistic" and decorative than forceful and rough. The tune always starts on a high C and works its way down to the flamenco E. Personally, I find it a strangely unsatisfying mixture—a sort of refined taranta, which is to say a contradiction in terms, though anything is good flamenco when sung by a good singer.

Its themes may concern the mines, but just as often they reflect the life of the *tartanero* (carter) and the *arriero* (muleteer), men who bring goods up from the ports or fish from the coast. The coastal mountains, however wild, are covered in a fine web of mule tracks.

The **murcianas, levantinas, arrieras del Campo de Dalías**, and other forms are all even more remotely derived from the taranta. They blend into folk song, and I only mention them for completeness: you are unlikely to hear them unless you take your holidays in those parts. Incidentally, the Campo de Dalías was the setting of the real-life events on which García Lorca based his *Bodas de sangre*. Let no one accuse him of realism: in that driest of dry lands there is nothing remotely resembling the forest in which he sets the murder.

◆ **Farruca and garrotín**
   Tracks 18 and 19

The farruca and garrotín are both folk songs adopted from northern Spain.

The **farruca** is above all a dance, and only performed by men. It appeared in the nineteenth century and probably came with the gangs of Galician workers brought in to work the labor-intensive cotton crops. In Gallego, the language of Galicia, *farruca* simply means a girl. It is plausible, or at any rate easy to imagine, that when the day's work was over and the laborers were back in the men's quarters of the vast *cortijos* (farmsteads), the Andalusians would start to sing; they almost always do. And equally plausible that the Galicians would want to join in with a song from their own land. The flamencos adopted it, flamencoized it, and put their own words to it, keeping only the word *farruca*.

The words are too trivial to be worth quoting, so perhaps it is not surprising that it is nearly always performed as a dance. Indeed, Tina Pavón, a fine singer, was so put off by the usual words that she decided to make hers celebrate the great Gypsy dancer from Seville known as El Farruco, who died recently. Just once I have heard it sung (by young Carmen Grilo) with such powerful *jondura* that the whole (flamenco) audience was gripped. But it was the singing only—the words turned out to be as trivial as ever.

The folk origins of the farruca show in its having a refrain (always to the same meaningless words, *tran tran tran treiro*), in its use of the minor scale, not the flamenco E mode, and in the regular, heavily accented beat of its slow 2/4 time. As with other song forms in our major and minor scales, the guitarist often keeps to a simple three-chord framework. It is played *por medio*, and the cadences often involve a little slide down through G and F-sharp to the chords on F, E, and A. The guitarist's falsetas often use the melody of the refrain. The verse varies in its tune, but you will almost always hear the long-held high note and the way it descends in groups of four notes to the end. Its strong and recent folk origins show in the fact that it *can* be written down as music, and still be recognizably akin to what you will hear.

I quote it in 2/4 time with some diffidence, because Paco Peña gives it as 4/4, and few men alive have his authority. But the 2/4 meter shows the emphatic and heavily accented beat that gives its style to the dance: there will be a short bit of zapateado, but in the main it consists of long slow steps, often with the foot poised and held off the ground, only to be brought down emphatically on the beat; or else a statuesque posing that then makes use of the beat to execute a sudden spin or other movement. Of the established dancers, Javier Barón manages somehow to infuse a sort of gleeful verve into its slow, deliberate progress, while Diego Llori does it with a statuesque restraint that conveys powerful rhythm in its very stillness. Another current exponent, Joaquín Cortés, seeks to turn the farruca into a form of modern ballet combined with the showmanship of the music hall: when he dances he likes to show his torso. It was the story going round the flamenco community that for Saura's film *Flamenco* he asked to do his farruca naked. Whether true or not, the story conveys their opinion of his exhibitionism.

The performance of the farruca on track 18 is by Juan Pinilla, accompanied by the guitarist Carlos Zárate. The words are not typical, either of the farruca or of flamenco. They clearly date from Franco's day. They are communist, more hopeful than realistic, and unlikely to mean much to the twenty-year-old singer. He probably chose them because he owes much to the man who wrote them and who spent years in prison without trial. So do I: this book is dedicated to him.

Like the farruca, the **garrotín** came with northern laborers (probably from Asturias) around 1900; it is in a major key and in common time, and it has a refrain—none of which features are flamenco. By the same token it needs no explaining, for a hearing is enough. It is seldom sung nowadays, and then usually for the dance—and even then, less often than the farruca.

I have heard one verse worth quoting. It pokes gentle fun at the *milor,* the noble English patron of yesteryear, who asks for the dance but gets its name wrong. The local transcription of "Yes, very well" has a savor all its own:

De Londres vino un inglés	From London came an Englishman
procedente de Londón	an Englishman from Londón.
me dijo, "yé berigüé	He said to me, "Yes, very well,
báileme usted un garrotón."	dance me a garrotón."
Ay garrotín, ay garrotán, *etc.*	Ay garrotín, ay garrotán, *etc.*

The performance of the garrotín on track 19 is by Lola La Cartujana, with the guitarist Carlos Zárate. She sings many song forms well, but not this one: she was unusually nervous—perhaps because of the room, the microphone, and the presence of a foreigner behind it. Normally the garrotín is sung (and danced) rather faster.

Her words, too, are less frivolous than usual:

Pregúntale a mi sombrero	Ask my hat
mi sombrero te dirá	my hat will tell you
las malas noches que paso	of the sleepless nights I spend
el relente que me das	driven out in the cold by you.
Ay garrotín, ay garrotán,	Ay garrotín, ay garrotán,
de la vera, vera, vera de San Juan.	on the eve of St. John.

✦ **Cantes de ida y vuelta: guajiras, rumbas, milongas, and colombianas**
Track 20

The cantes de ida y vuelta are songs from Latin America. The phrase means "songs of going there and back," which stems from the theory that they were brought back from the Americas by flamencos who had crossed the Atlantic. The guajiras (then known as *puntos de Habana*) arrived in the 1840s and the rumbas about 1900, both from Cuba. The milongas (and vidalitas) were brought from Argentina a few years later. The colombianas got their name not from their country of origin, but from the name of a song.

To my mind they are none of them flamenco, except in the touch they get from being sung by flamencos. But Spain and flamenco have been influenced by Latin American music just as the rest of Europe has been influenced by transatlantic black music. Cuba has been more influential than most, because war with the United States in 1898 meant that a lot of Andalusian conscripts were there. So the rumbas and guajiras are commonest, but you will also hear others occasionally.

It is a point worth making that nearly all flamenco has origins outside Andalusia. The question is when it came in and how much it has adapted. The intensely flamenco tarantas developed from the folkloric fandango, which came from the Moors in the Middle Ages; the villancicos have been around since the middle ages too, yet are still no more than barely flamen-coized—and even then only by the singer's style. The rhythms, melody, and harmonies of the *guajiras* seem to me to be so fixed that they are almost anti-flamenco, but the same could be said of the verdiales from which Juan Breva's fandango developed, which in turn led to the very flamenco mala-gueñas. However, this process of transformation is less likely to occur today —in our era of television, radio, and recordings, because these have on music a similar effect to that which printing had on language, that of fixing it and slowing down change.

The **guajira** has a lovely lilting tune and makes a very good dance for such graceful exponents of the old school as Merché Esmeralda, who has been a flamenco beauty for many years—and still is. Saura was well advised to get her to dance the guajira in his film *Flamenco*. Shawl, fans, grace, ele-gance—the lot. I have seen the guajira done by a dancer who chose to dress in her idea of how a Cuban peasant maid might look. As she moved, the ends of the kerchief she had tied round her head wobbled and flopped, so that she looked more like a demented rabbit. Somehow the grace of the dance did not come across.

The word *guajira* means "girl" in Yucateca, the native Indian language of Cuba. Actually, *guajiro* meant lord, *señor, monsieur.* But the soldiers in Cuba used it for anyone, and girl it is.

The words of the song are in *décimas*—ten-line verses with the rhyme scheme *abbaa ccddc.* Such sophistication is unknown in flamenco but not uncommon in Latin America. They always tell of some delectable Cuban maiden.

The music is in the major mode of our Western music, with the time sig-nature 6/8 + 3/4 (as is the petenera). This fits with the flamenco twelve-count as

I . . I . . I . I . I .

The pleasure of the song lies partly in the freedom of the voice, which lingers on a high note before curling over and falling by a six-note interval. This lingering creates variety within the slow lilt of the song by dragging the rhythm. Meanwhile, the guitar maintains its arpeggios in a monotonous three-chord sequence and pulls on the rhythm to vary the commonplace vamp that betrays the song's folk-song origin.

The performance of the guajira on track 20 is by Sensi, with Carlos Zárate on guitar. The words of the first verse follow the ten-line verse pattern (décima) with the scheme described earlier, though in assonance, not rhyme.

¡Ay! contigo me caso Indiana	Indian girl, I'm going to marry you.
¡Ay! si se entera tu papa	If your daddy discovers it
y se lo dice a tu mama	and tells your mama,
¡Ay! hermosísima Cubana	gorgeous Cuban girl, [tell them]
tengo una casa en La Habana	I have a house in Havana
reservada para ti	ready for you
con el techo de marfil	with an ivory ceiling
y el piso de plataforma	and a raised floor
para ti, blanca paloma,	and, my little white dove,
llevo yo la flor de lis.	I'm bringing you a lily.

The detail of the raised floor, as though it were on a par with the ivory ceiling, suggests these words are old and authentic: before air conditioning, this was a luxurious way of keeping a house cool.

We see another pattern in her second verse:

Me gusta por la mañana	I like to spend the morning
después del café bebío	when I've finished my coffee
pasearme por La Habana	strolling around Havana
con un cigarro encendío	smoking a cigar.
y comprarme un papelón	I buy one of those broadsheets

de esos que llaman diario	they call a "newspaper"
que parezca un millonario	so I look like a millionaire
rico de la población.	a rich man about town.

Fun, but I doubt its authenticity.

The **rumba** also came from Cuba and is even less flamenco than the guajira, since the latter has a flamenco form of dance to it and a flamenco twelve-count to follow, while the rumba remains fundamentally popular Latin American music for the dance floor, with sexily ostentatious movements of the hips and body. It had a complicated rhythm in Cuba but spread to the United States and Europe in a rhythmically simpler form: with slight variations this consists of a constantly repeated guitar rhythm: I II I I.

The tunes are in the major, minor, or (very occasionally) flamenco E mode. In the 1950s it seems to have been taken up by the Barcelona Gypsies and is still a popular dance at fiestas in Spain today. It was very popular on the dance floors of Europe and the United States until the 1970s, when it was overtaken by its derivatives, the mambo and the chachachá. Paco de Lucía transformed it in the 1970s, and since then it has been adopted by popular pseudo-flamenco groups such as the Gypsy Kings, whose popularity (outside Andalusia) has helped to promote such a false image of flamenco.

The **milonga** is a type of folk song from the Plate River area in Argentina, where it is still very popular. The song is very ornate, in common (4/4) time, starting high and with its long held notes mixed with the complicated weavings and wanderings of the voice. It is in the minor, but the verse ends on a major third (what musicians call the Picardy third), after which the refrain, if there is one, stays in the major.

The guitar is played entirely picado (that is, with no flamenco rasgueado), and its falsetas are often as ornate as the song.

The words are usually in eight-line verses with the rhyme scheme *abab* or *abba*, although because they tell a story (often a sentimental one about dying soldiers or lost loves), I have heard it sung to the ballad form of four-line stanzas, with assonance on the even lines throughout. Like all Latin American songs, its 4/4 rhythms tend to be given a lilt by the performers' advance or delay of the second beat of the bar. (The Viennese waltz, at least as the Viennese themselves play it, achieves a similar lilt in its rhythm by slightly advancing the second beat of its three-beat bar.)

Until recently the **colombiana** was not often performed, and the old recordings I had heard did not compel attention. But it is coming back. Like the guajira, it has a lilting tune in a major key that is characterized by long-held notes and the fact that it ends on the third note of the scale. Again like the guajira, the guitar accompaniment is in simple harmonies, in 4/4 time, to an unvaried rhythm: Ⅰ ⅠⅠ Ⅰ Ⅰ. The words are usually in a six-line verse with the rhyme scheme *ababab* and are sentimental. They address a Colombian girl, often ending on the refrain *Oye mi voz, Colombiana* (Listen to me, Colombiana).

In summary, these Latin American songs may be sung by flamencos, but none entirely escape being what they are: Latin American songs. None are in the flamenco mode; hardly any escape words of saccharine emotion; hardly any have anything more interesting than a basic three-chord accompaniment; and none (not even the guajira) have the force, the bite, the *pellizco*, that characterizes flamenco. Even the guajira, with its metric scheme that fits the flamenco twelve-count, makes a dance that is graceful but never forceful. I don't remember ever seeing a Gypsy dancing it.

✦ Zambras: zambras, alboreás, moscas, and cachuchas

There are two types of **zambra**. One belongs to the Sacromonte, the steep mountainside behind Granada, where the Gypsies used to live, mostly in caves, until they were forced to leave them some forty years ago. Some of these caves are known as zambras and are still used for performance. All performers sit round at one end of the cave and support the singer or leader, who whips up the festive atmosphere. The Sacromonte style of song and dance is characterized by its cheerful, upbeat pace and the electric energy of its dancing. Pretty well everything turns into a stampede of clapping and zapateo. Most of its rhythms are the upbeat 2/4 time of the tango. Occasionally you will hear the 3/4 meter of one or other of the local fandangos—probably the *fandango del Albaicín*—but done at speed. All is noise, color, swirling festivity, and machine-gun rhythms. I feel the need to add that in watching Granadan Gypsies dance, I am intensely aware of their stony hard eyes: there is festivity, yes, but there is nothing affable about it. The eyes seem to convey contempt for the payo they are performing to, and this gives the zambra a hard edge. In Granada, the only word they use for the non-Gypsy is the derogatory *payo*, never *gachó*.

The word *zambra* comes from the Arabic for music (*zámara*), though some think it refers to the flute (*zamr*). But it would probably be wrong to describe it as a Moorish fiesta. As long ago as 1567, one Moor protested that "I don't know how people can say so: no good Moor ever attended these things, and the *alfaquís* would leave as soon as the musicians began to play or sing. . . . We don't have these zambras in Africa or Turkey; it's a local custom." ("Turkey" is mentioned because this quote dates from the time of the Turkish Ottoman Empire, which dominated all Arab states. The *alfaquí* is a doctor of Koranic law.) The word's Arabic origin and the song form's very Gypsy style go to support the theory that the persecuted Moriscos (Moors who converted to Christianity in order to stay in Spain) went to hide out among the Gypsies.

The other kind of zambra is the song and dance of a traditional Gypsy wedding. This would include any of the festive song forms, together with the **alboreá**, discussed earlier in this chapter, and others such as the mosca and cachucha. The **mosca** (fly) is a dance in which four women make sweeping gestures down their skirts, as though brushing away flies. The **cachucha** is in 6/8 time and in the major; its meaning is suggested by the words:

147

La cachucha de mi mare	My mother's cachucha
es más grande que la mía	is bigger than mine
que se la vi ayer tarde	I saw it last night
cuando se quedó dormía	when she was asleep
ven a mí, ven a mí	come to me, come to me,
junto a mi vera, ven a mí.	come next to me, come.

The light-heartedness of it is taken further by the next verse:

La cachucha de mi pare	My father's cachucha
se le ha llevaíto el viento, *etc.*	has gone with the wind, *etc.*

◆ **Songs influenced by flamenco: saetas, villancicos, sevillanas, campanilleros, bamberas, nanas, pregones, temporeras, and cantes de trilla**
Track 21

The **saeta** is a song of passionate devotion to Christ or the Virgin—the word means "arrow"—sung to tableaux (*pasos*) that are carried through the streets during the Holy Week processions. These pasos are massive and sometimes present whole scenes of the Passion, with many life-sized figures. Each paso is served by its brotherhood, which is a sort of club, rather like a Masonic lodge, devoted to its (expensive) upkeep and to supplying the carriers. Over the whole day, they will need more than one crew of up to fifty men to carry, and each paso has its accompanying band.

The saetas were not originally flamenco. They were sung first by Franciscan friars and then by any specautor who might feel moved to express his grief at the Crucifixion. Flamenco singers adopted them and gave them toná tunes. They have now lost some of their former spontaneity: the paso stops at agreed points on the route where the saeta is sung by professonals, either *por siguiriya* or else *por martinete*—that is to say, in free rhythm but following the melodic line of either song form. The style of singing varies from city to city.

The saetas somehow lose their quality when sung for recording, so track 21 is one I recorded during an Easter procession. It is of poor quality because I had no means of shrouding the mike from wind noises—as it was, I was lucky to be asked up to the balcony with the singer. I asked an old hand where this saeta was from and was told wryly that he thought it came from somewhere on the road about halfway between Jerez and Seville: the singer was young and inexperienced. You will notice the long-held notes sung a quarter tone flat—and the public appreciation of them.

Originally any peasant song (*canto de villano*), the **villancico** has long since come to mean a Christmas carol, as sung all over Spain. In Andalusia it has developed into the *zambomba*. This is an occasion for meeting in the week or so before Christmas to sing carols, especially, but not exclusively, among Gypsies. The zambomba itself is a drum with a stick through the membrane that when moved up and down produces a sound somewhere between a drone and a drumbeat. It is also used during the Rocío pilgrimage in singing hymns in sevillana form to the Virgin. The Gypsies light fires on the patios and sit round them to sing, a scene that Saura tried to recreate with lighting in his film. The tunes are of all sorts and rhythms, most commonly in 3/4 time, though sometimes as tientos, bulerías, or even rumbas. I give the words of one, sung as a tiento, which I chose because it may reflect something of the strong emotion aroused among the Gypsies at Christmas and Easter. In Holy Week the statues from the two Gypsy parishes of Jerez, the Christ of the Arrest (*el Prendimiento*) in Santiago and the dying Christ (*la Expiración*) from San Telmo in the parish of San Miguel are greeted with fervor as they emerge from the church. I have seen Gypsy girls almost swooning, like our adolescents before a pop star, as they greet the Christ with cries of *guapo!* (pretty!).

Envidia tiene la rosa del color	The rose envies the color
de su carita divina	of his divine little face
y yo estoy viendo en la frente de	but I can see on the forehead of
mi Dios	my God
una corona de espinas	a crown of thorns
¡Qué dolor!¡ Qué dolor!	Oh, what grief! What grief!
Una corona de espinas.	a crown of thorns.
Pastores de la Laguna	Shepherds of the Lake
ponerse to's a cantar.	sing to him all.
El niño que está en la cuna	The child in the cradle
en una cruz morirá.	will die on a cross.
Envidia, *etc.*	The rose, *etc.*
María dale cobijo	Mary give him shelter
y cúbrelo con tu manto	shield him with your cloak
pa' que no vea tu hijo	so your child cannot see
la tarde del viernes santo.	Good Friday afternoon.
Envidia, *etc.*	The rose, *etc.*
La noche de nochebuena	On Christmas Eve
ponerse to's a cantar	let us all sing
que esa carita morena	so that little Gypsy face
sonríe por no llorar.	may smile and not weep.
Envidia, *etc.*	The rose, *etc.*

Others have a more local flavor. The Three Kings are the Catholic equivalent of Santa Claus in that they bring the presents. The following extract has a certain charm:

Reyes, Reyes Magos,
que no tengo juguetes
porque soy gitano.
Y si pasan por Santiago
yo vivo en la calle Nueva.
Yo dejo mi ventana abierta
por si vienen, por si pasan.

Kings, Wise Kings,
I have no toys
because I'm a Gypsy.
And if you come by Santiago:
I live on New Street.
I'll leave my window open
in case you come this way.

The **sevillanas** are not flamenco. When danced at fiestas, they are usually played by a band; they may be sung in chorus; they keep to a strict 3/4 rhythm; they are danced in pairs; and they are choreographed. None of this belongs to flamenco. The sevillana is in fact an Andalusian form of the seguidilla, a Castilian folk dance that when it went upmarket developed into the bolero, and when it went south became the faster sevillanas. But—and this is a big "but"—they became so popular, and deservedly so, that they have been flamencoized in various ways, including the dancers' arm and hand movements. As a graceful Spanish-style dance it became the *sevillanas boleras*; it is danced and sung to appropriate words on the pilgrimage to the Virgin of the Dew (*rocío*) as the *sevillana rociera* (which is why you will see it danced in boots—the pilgrims have to cope with sand dunes and marshes); and you will hear it sung to stories from the Bible as the *sevillana biblica*. But, above all, it is danced at fiestas.

The un-flamenco nature of the dance shows most in its choreography: it has at least nine different steps combined in a set order, but which varies within each of the four parts of the dance. All in all, this comes to a permutation of more than forty-two steps, all preestablished. This adds up to all the swirling grace of an old dance—say, a highly choreographed Viennese waltz—and yet it can be sensual to the point of erotic. This may seem a strange thing to say of a dance where the partners never touch. But the girl gyrates round the man gracefully, sinuously, and flirtily, and if she is good her arms and hands remain the whole time within an inch or two of him, as though she were caressing him without actually touching, until the last note, when the man puts his arm round the girl's waist. Here I add the heretical comment that I think the sevillanas better when the man is not a professional dancer. When he is, it becomes ingenious choreography; when he is not, the dance gains from his restraint: he becomes a still point of focus for the woman to gyrate around and relate to. And the flamenco dress comes into its own here, with its frills and furbelows, its swirling skirt and bright colors.

The tune can be in the major, minor, or Andalusian scale, but it is always in 3/4 time. A most surprising aspect of it is that the dancer comes in with the basic sevillana step, but on an upbeat.

I would strongly recommend Carlos Saura's documentary *Sevillanas*, which is available as a video. It does not really show the dance as you would see it in a fiesta. Instead, you see it done solo by some great dancers. But it rings some surprising changes—some of them enchanting—and for guitarists it offers the treat of an astonishing display in duet by Paco de Lucía and Manolo Sanlúcar.

I will merely identify the remainder of the songs that I have mentioned—the campanilleros, bamberas, nanas, pregones, temporeras, and cantes de trilla—as they are not common and this is an introduction to flamenco, not an encyclopedia.

Campanilleros are songs originally of a religious brotherhood who went to prayers to the sound of hand bells—hence the name, which means "bell-ringers." It has kept its religious theme. The melody is in the minor, sung in 6/8 time at a slow, almost dead-march tempo. The verse scheme is fairly complicated: six and a half eleven-syllable lines, the half being one five-syllable line in the middle, giving roughly the rhyme scheme *abab(b)ab*. Thus the only flamenco aspect of it is the singer's style.

Bamberas are songs for swings. Unlike the campanilleros, they are entirely flamenco. The tune uses the whole Andalusian scale but stays mainly within the five notes A–E at the upper end of the scale before tumbling down to low E. It is this constant drop to the flamenco cadence, rather than the song's rhythm, that suggests the swing's return. The words suggest that the girl on the swing is no longer a child.

Nanas are lullabyes. The only ones I have heard have been in 4/4 time, mainly in A minor with a drop down to Andalusian E.

Pregones are street vendors' songs, usually in free rhythm and unaccompanied.

Temporeras and **cantes de trilla** are songs of the farm—harvesting and threshing songs. You might hear them in the fields, but I have heard only one flamenco perform them.

6

Where Is Flamenco Heading?

They dance very well nowadays, but they should perhaps be a bit careful with their innovations.

PILAR LÓPEZ, A GREAT DANCER, IN HER NINETIES

It will help if I first put the matter in context. During the first half of the regime of General Franco (1940–55), flamenco was driven by hunger and contempt back to its roots, back to being the music of the outcasts, of those who survived as best they could on the fringes of society or outside it. This was the period known in Spain as the Years of Hunger—no empty phrase, considering that in those years some 25,000 Spaniards starved to death. Faced with economic collapse, Franco was forced to hand affairs over to the technocrats—to put competent men in place of the political yes-men who had made up his government hitherto. This was in about 1960, when tourists were first allowed in, with the first package holidays to the new coastal resorts. And here lies its relevance to us, for with the tourists came the tourist tablaos and the kitsch flamenco they purveyed. Managers of hotels and tablaos found they could entertain their customers for little outlay by choosing a dancer for her pretty face or sexy manner, rather than for her talent. The customers didn't know any better, or perhaps that was even what they wanted. A bright flounced dress, a few wiggles to the sound of castanets and foot stamping, a bit of strumming on the guitar, a voice wailing in roughly the right direction—these were all that was needed. It was colorful and sounded *típico*. This "flamenco" served up in tourist hotels was and is a shoddy parody of the real thing, and it came near to destroying flamenco by debasing it. It gave the idea to many foreigners, then and now, that this was what flamenco *is*. To most Spaniards, at that time, flamenco was in any case the low-class noisemaking of those layabout southerners. And the visitor had little chance of learning that any other sort existed. Not the least of its harmful effects is that, in Britain at least, many still think so today. An acquaintance of mine expressed surprise that I should be interested in Carmen Miranda with fruit on her head . . .

And yet . . . and yet the tablaos, much reviled by flamencos, almost saved the other flamenco—the flamenco of ancestral memory—by giving employment to professionals. Where else could they earn their living? Many of the finest singers and dancers performing today had their first chance in them. They still do that service today: I have seen promising talents there. And even though what they are doing is often tatty, it enables them to earn a living while practicing or developing their technique. In the late 1950s and the 1960s, either you found a job in a tablao, or you emigrated to where there was work. Or you starved.

The following extract gives an idea of what life was like for many Andalusians. It is from "Los Andaluces," a poem published in 1964 by José Hierro, a poet from the north coast. The three places mentioned in the third stanza were sites of prisons notorious in Franco's day:

Decían: "Ojú, qué frío";	They said: "Oy! how cold!"
no "Qué espantoso, tremendo,	not "What frightful, terrible,
injusto, inhumano frío."	unjust, inhuman cold!"
Resignadamente: "Ojú,	Just resignedly: "Oy!
qué frío . . ." Los andaluces . . .	how cold . . ." The Andalusians . . .

En dónde habrían dejado
sus jacas; en dónde habrían
dejado su sol, su vino,
sus olivos, sus salinas.
En dónde habrían dejado
su odio . . . Parecían hechos
de indiferencia, pobreza,
latigazo . . . "Ojú, qué frío."

Wherever they may have left
their mares; wherever they left
their sunshine, their wine,
their olive groves and salt pans.
Wherever they may have left
their hatred . . . They seemed now
only indifferent, poor,
and whipped . . . "Oy! How cold!"

Tiritaban bajo ropas
delgadas, telas tejidas
para cantar y morir
siempre al sol. Y las llevaban
para callar y vivir
al frío de Ocaña y Burgos
al viento helado del mar
del Dueso . . . Los andaluces . . .

They shivered in flimsy clothes,
woven for singing and dying
under the ever-blazing sun.
Now, they wore them
to be mute, and living
in the cold of Ocaña and Burgos,
in the freezing sea winds
of the Dueso . . . The Andalusians . . .

The kitsch flamenco of tourism may be a matter of supply and demand, and thus the fault of the tourists. But it is certainly also that of the tablao managers and their contemptuous assumptions. The trouble is, they tend to carry the same mentality when they tour abroad. Corazón Flamenco, who came to London in 1995–6, brought the great artist Manuela Carrasco, but the first hour of the show was made tedious with kitsch—and what is worse, kitsch performed by good artists. They must have decided that unless they softened us up with touristy stuff we wouldn't accept Manuela Carrasco. I hope the scathing reviews were translated for them. I reviewed it for an Andalusian magazine and made the point that quality would always be recognized. By trying to make it "accessible" to us, they had debased their art and reinforced the impression, already widespread in Britain, that flamenco is tinsel.

Sometime before the coming of democracy in 1975, two things helped spur the rebirth of real flamenco. One was a massive recorded anthology, *Magna antología del cante flamenco*, published in 1955, that brought together a large number of surviving recordings. It marked a turning point in the respect it showed for this music, unique in Europe, whose roots go back so far. The recordings brought back from the dead the singers and players of previous generations and made them available as models to a younger generation. The other help came from the setting up of singing competitions throughout Andalusia. Neither has anything to do with entertainment or holds any interest for the general public. But the competitions are very well attended by people who had not had much chance to hear flamenco sung other than unaccompanied in the fields or in the workshop. And the aspiring singers who competed were given thus the opportunity to have a professional guitarist accompany them. It contributed to a revival of good flamenco song. Song is the heart of flamenco and preceded the more widely known performance art of dance, so this revival was not publicly recognized, other than among flamencos themselves. But it went on and it is still going on. From that time onward dates a steady rise of quality flamenco, going hand in hand with a growing awareness that this is an interesting indigenous culture, a widespread one, and not to be ignored. For years now flamenco has been on the rise. Today it is flourishing more perhaps than it has ever done.

The poverty of Franco's Spain has gone, and with prosperity has come an enormous rise in communication. In the 1950s and 1960s, the ordinary Andalusian used the train to emigrate, to avoid starvation by going to where there might be work—Bilbao or Barcelona (Catalonia came to be known as the ninth Andalusian province). Or else, usually by a long foot-slog, they made the journey to the Costas, where, from 1960 on, tourism had a phenomenal increase. John Hooper tells of the culture shock suffered by the young and hungry Andalusian peasant when confronted with the luxury, the chrome and glass, the unimagined wealth, and (not least) the exposed flesh of the package tourists: when Málaga's general hospital enlarged its psychiatric wing, it became known as "waiters' ward."

I have heard it suggested that the tragic heart of cante jondo, the ancestral memory of persecution and starvation, must dwindle into triviality because the Gypsies are no longer persecuted and no longer starving. This seems nonsense to me. Prosperity is no impediment to the jondo tradition, for people still have occasion to feel marginalized, deprived, deserted, or jilted. Or to be imprisoned: this seems to be as good an occasion as any for keeping the carceleras alive.

But in today's relative prosperity, together with food and clothing has come closer communication—through the bus, the car, and above all, overwhelmingly, radio, television, and commercial recordings. This is bound to affect flamenco profoundly and permanently. The music of the outcasts was performed away from the public ear until the nineteenth century. It first gained an audience with the cafés cantantes of the late nineteenth century and became known outside Spain only in the twentieth century, when promoters pushed the tinselly element, encouraged appropriately trite versions of the music, and brought in dancing stars such as La Argentina—fine dancers, but bailarines rather than bailaoras. This was show business on the Hollywood model. Meanwhile, in Andalusia, the flamencos went on as they had before, singing and playing in the style they had learned from their elders.

Under today's conditions, the singer, whose ancestors would have known only the other singers of his immediate area, will know how others are changing the songs in every area not only of Andalusia, but of Madrid and Barcelona too. That is the first effect. The second is that flamenco is being bombarded with pop music, and the younger flamencos are influenced more and more by it, as well as by rock, jazz, and the music of Latin America.

Chapter 6

This cultural bombardment from outside is reinforced by a trend from within. For forty years Franco had run the country in the belief that outside influences were pollutants. He referred to the legacy of liberalism as "bastard, Frenchified, Europeanizing." (In his mind this was a crescendo of abuse: "bastard" being the mildest of these terms). The Spanish people were to be kept pure by his shutting out of all outside influences. So the coming of democracy and freedom was accompanied by a thirst to find links with the outside world, with other cultures, and with peoples long since expelled from Spain. Hence various attempts to find connections between flamenco and the music of the Mahgreb, or with Egyptian or Arab or Jewish music. Hence also the desire of the young to "plug in" to the wider world of rock, by playing and singing what they call fusion.

The trouble with fusion is that it doesn't fuse. Flamenco rock is rock music tinged with flamenco mannerisms. The mannerisms don't alter the fact that it is fundamentally rock. To see this, you need only look to rock's steady beat, which is alien to flamenco and incompatible with its compás. I have been told that in some countries there is debate over the use of percussion in flamenco. This baffled me, for in six years of living among flamencos I had never heard of it. Perhaps because percussion belongs to rock, pop, and jazz, people who play these naturally use it. It does not belong to flamenco, unless you wish to make it a question of mere words. This point was made by the great singer José Mercé (who has himself included some jazz and salsa in his recordings): "It seems that all music is flamenco now. You cannot fool people, saying that jazz and salsa are flamenco." For me, and for flamencos, what happens in rock music, whether fusion or not, is another subject.

The same applies to fusion with jazz, even though the sheer musicianship of Paco de Lucía, who plays with such jazz notables as John McLaughlin, Chick Corea, and Al DiMeola, might make one hesitate. His own verdict is instructive and authoritative: "Fusion may come to something, though I don't believe in it. In the work I've done with Corea, McLaughlin, or Di-Meola, the music was neither flamenco nor jazz: it was a fusion of musicians rather than of music."

The various attempts to fuse flamenco with the music of the Mahgreb work the other way round—it stays flamenco, and the North African part of the input only works at all so long as the artists agree to do everything in the one rhythm they share: the 2/4 time of the flamenco tango. The widely popular couple Lole and Manuel tried at first to link their music with the Mahgreb by singing in Arabic—justifiably, for Lole was born there and speaks the language—and many of their earlier songs were in the tango rhythm. But Lole soon came to the decision that the two styles had nothing else in common.

Flamenco-rock fusion, which is by far the most widespread, is faced with a further problem, since it contains a contradiction. It is the essence of pop of any sort that it be in fashion. The very words used to describe this—"with it," "in," "hep," "hip," and so on—came from that world. And the fact that the words themselves have to change with the fashion indicates just how essential it is that it *not* have anything to do with yesterday. Yet the essence of flamenco is its tradition, handed down from generation to generation, which does *not* mean, as the flamencologists seem to think, that it must stay what it was. It evolves. The advent of every powerful performer influences it, changes it to some extent: Chacón yesterday, Morente today; Ramón Montoya yesterday, Paco de Lucía today; and we have already seen that Carmen Amaya's dancing has influenced every woman dancer ever since. Indeed, it has evolved so much that it is unlikely today's flamencos would even recognize much of the music played and sung in 1800. What, for example, would today's flamencos make of their Gypsy predecessors in Triana holding hands in a ring, dancing to the music of the "English Branle"? But the very word *evolution* implies something that grows out of what went before. In this respect flamenco is like sherry to rock fusion's Coca-Cola. What goes into the bottle of sherry is a blend of all vintages produced since the firm set up its *solera*: some of what you drink will be from a relatively recent harvest, while a small part, maybe only a few molecules, may be more than a century old. Just so, as we have already seen, some of the ingredients of the siguiriya go back to primitive music, to what T. S. Eliot described as "the backward half-look, over the shoulder, towards the primitive terror"; while the cantes de ida y vuelta, with their Cuban influences, were the fusion of a century ago. Within rock, on the other hand, lies the urge to be new—different from what was produced by those old farts of last year. In that respect it is some other drink, new to the market, that aims to *replace* Coke—not to evolve out of it, or to improve it.

The flamenco rock group Ketama may be said to have had the musical ability, the persistence, and the success to influence things. But by the time they gained a wide hearing, they were being promoted by an English recording company and complaining that they were better appreciated in England than in their own country. In other words, their music, however good it might be, had effectively begun to move out of the flamenco world.

It seems likely that elements of rock, jazz, and pop will enter the flamenco world if the singers involved are good enough to have more than momentary influence. But the greater danger may well come from the recording companies. I would not go down the street to hear Estrella Morente sing, since I don't like pop. But millions do, and the newspaper reviewers rave over what they call her flamenco. Her second CD has netted her about $120,000 as of this writing, and sales continue. Her famous father, Enrique Morente, could never have come near such a figure. Nor could any authentic flamenco. Unlike Joaquín Cortés, she did not set her sights on fortune at all costs. But is it surprising that young singers such as she go for such sums? Navajita Plateá, a successful fusion group, has a singer, Pelé, who can sing good, authentic flamenco. But he doesn't, at least not in public, because he earns so much more by singing his brand of fusion.

Where Is Flamenco Heading?

Some of the ingredients of fusion seem likely to stay. The box drum seems a natural extension of clapping and tapping. And the use of the flute, which emerged from the flamencos' search for their Moorish origins, may stay, too. Otherwise, the staying power of such novelties will depend less on what they do than on the caliber of the performer and his influence on other flamencos.

Flamencos themselves have the same problem coming to terms with this changing world, as every older generation does with the habits of its young. In this instance it means getting used to their offspring playing flamenco rock fusion. You could say that this is part of the recurring spiral of history, wherein ever since Abraham came out of Ur of the Chaldees, youth has been said by its elders (and, of course, betters) to be going to the dogs. Yet there is a possibility that this may not be so, that the music may not survive what amounts to a radical and nonrecurring change in the historical circumstances. For the people who make flamenco are no longer outcasts harried by the law, the church, or penury. Again, you don't have to be poor and persecuted in order to feel sad or happy, and the Andalusian finds it natural to let his feelings come out in song. Even when he is not one to find his own words, there are enough verses for every mood:

No hay penilla ni alegría
que se quede sin cantar.
Por eso hay más cantares
que gotas de agua en el mar
y arena en los arenales.

There is no sorrow or joy
that isn't sung.
That's why there are more songs
than drops of water in the sea
and grains of sand on the beach.

Perhaps the greater danger lies in our commercialized monoculture in which Brazilians, Japanese, Eskimos, and Germans all eat Big Macs while listening to the same music, dressed in the same jeans. I fear I was cheering a losing rear guard when the opening of the first McDonald's in Rome provoked a mass demonstration with placards that read "Food sí! Fast no!"

There is one effect of modern prosperity which I do deplore. Perhaps influenced by the conventions of pop music, it has become the custom to put a microphone before every singer and guitarist on every occasion, however small the venue. Such amplifying depersonalizes and hardens the singer's voice. It also makes it deafening. They tell me it is necessary because the audience makes too much noise. This is a chicken-and-egg explanation. In a small club room, with the sound blasting out, audiences that used to talk now shout. When, as sometimes happens, a singer stands and comes forward from the microphone, the effect is to switch off the sound—and it usually shuts the audience up. Because they are no longer being blasted with noise, they listen.

Nearly all this speculation over the future of flamenco concerns the song. It is important to keep this separate in one's mind from the dance, where experiment is a different matter. Song is essentially the expression of the singer's feelings, which may also be a performance art; dance is essentially a performance art, which may also express the dancer's feelings. But as dance is the part of flamenco that belongs first and foremost to the world of public entertainment, it has always moved with the times and fashions.

The significance of this distinction between performance and expression emerges when we notice that in the song today, one of the most destructive influences is that of the established singer who gives his performance, takes his money, and moves on to his next engagement. I have seen a fiesta ruined by this routine singing. When the singer is not committed, emotionally and totally, what he does is public performance and nothing more. In flamenco circles I find myself one of a growing number who would rather hear an unknown man sing in a bar, without guitar and without especial talent, careless of whether anyone is listening, simply because he feels the need to express himself in song, than listen to an established star giving a routine performance because that is what he has been paid to do. Even if the performing singer has artistic integrity, he still faces the performer's problem of starting at a prearranged date and time: if he is not in the mood (and cannot conjure it up), he just has to do his best. The result will not be good flamenco, only an honest attempt. Indeed, this can apply to the dance, too. There was an amusing instance in a flamenco locale one evening, when a party of eight or ten Gypsies came in to sit round a table for a *tapa* and a drink. One was a young dancer called Rin, a *mote* (nickname) he got as a child when he was a devotee of Rin Tin Tin comics. A young woman started to sing bulerías, and it was clear she was trying—maybe a bit too hard and too obviously—to get Rin to dance. Knuckles tapped the table, but Rin sat on, beer in hand. Then a girl at the far end of the table began to sing. She was wretchedly thin and poorly dressed, with downcast eyes and a downtrodden look; her voice was a thin thread of sound; and she was patently singing only for herself. The reaction was immediate. Something about her song got to Rin and compelled him to jump up and dance to her singing.

But this is rare. A singer can sing for himself; a dancer is a performer above all. And today, quite apart from the ballet of tutus and tippy-toes, dance flourishes in such varied forms that the flamenco-influenced dance known to most through the Saura films (*Carmen*, *Bodas de sangre*, and *El amor brujo*) is just one more form of dance in a world buzzing with successful creativity. Fine flamenco dancers such as Sara Baras and Antonio Canales are moving more and more into the world of modern dance. They make their performances a sort of dance fusion and are widely popular and successful. But they are leaving the world of authentic flamenco behind, leaving it to such consecrated goddesses as Manuela Carrasco and Juana Amaya. Luckily, others of the younger generation continue to dance pure flamenco, chief among them Eva Yerbabuena and her prizewinning followers Mercedes Ruiz and Andrés Peña.

There is growing worldwide interest in modern dance and in ethnic dance, if the word *ethnic* may be applied properly to the Irish of *Riverdance*, Australians stomping in boots, various guys named Mo, and other such suc-

Figure 24. Sara Baras, dancer. Photo: Juan Gallego. Courtesy of *El Olivo* Magazine

cesses. Among all these, the work of Sara Baras and the films of Carlos Saura are just two more manifestations of a thriving, booming art form, one that is essentially performance art.

So will today's developments kill the authentic flamenco of tradition? Many of the old guard believe so. I don't. All these questions and speculations refer mainly to the professionals, the public performers, such as are contracted to recording companies, together with such would-be Michael

Figure 25. Eva Yerbabuena, dancer. Photo: Carlos Rico. Courtesy of
El Olivo Magazine

Figure 26. Mercedes Ruiz, Córdoba prizewinner. Courtesy of the artist

Figure 27. Andrés Peña, prizewinner in Seville. Courtesy of the artist

Jacksons as Joaquín Cortés. If these people are flourishing, it is because flamenco is flourishing as it has not done in two hundred years. What these successful performers are doing—or at least, those among them with the artistic gifts to go beyond mere fashion (I exclude Joaquín Cortés)—will certainly influence flamenco and make it evolve. But they are not its source. Today most of the real thing is performed by flamencos for their own kind, in the street, in the home, in village peñas, or in the flamenco-dominated towns of the Seville-Cádiz axis. While this groundswell continues to flourish, the traditional art will not die. Only if these ordinary people lose interest, then flamenco will be a dodo anyway and go where dodos go, into the museum, which is to say into the mausoleum. For the moment there is no sign of this. You can hear more people singing in the traditional way today than you could fifteen years ago, just as you can hear more fusion with rock and jazz. Both are symptoms of the flourishing.

7

Who Are the Gypsies of Andalusia?

Her people
are assembled in her bones,
She's their summation.
NORMAN McCAIG, "AN OLD HIGHLAND WOMAN"

To enjoy flamenco music, you do not have to know about the persecution of the Jews, the expulsion of the Moors, and the centuries-long marginalization of the Gypsies; but it does help to know that these things happened, and that the whole wretched story underlies the trembling grief of the song—even though the singer himself may not realize it.

In Britain we tend to confuse Gypsies with "travelers" of any sort, who in my country are often descended from the Irish "navvies," the canal and railway workers who came over in the nineteenth century. The Gypsies are a distinct ethnic group, with a language of their own, one so clearly descended from Sanskrit that it demonstrates their Indian origin. Who and where in India, and why and when they emigrated—these are still matters for debate. But I find myself convinced of the who and where by an experience in Granada. I happened to be with an Indian friend, Eire, a lecturer at an American university, who asked me where she might be able to see a Gypsy and how she would recognize him. We were going to see the Charterhouse monastery, which is in a suburb where many of them live, so I told her there would be no problem. Two Gypsies boarded our bus, women of

Figure 28. María Soleá. Though she no longer sings, she reminds me of what a flamenco said of El Farruco: "My dear, people should pay, just to see that face." Photo: Miguel Angel González. Courtesy of the Centro Andaluz de Flamenco

the older generation, in traditional dress, who had been selling sprigs of heather and telling fortunes outside the cathedral. They stared long and fascinated at Eire, who was wearing a sari. Then one turned to me and said, *Es de las nuestras* (she is one of us). When we got off the bus, Eire said, "They? Gypsy? They're Sindhi!" I asked what the Sindhi were like and was told they had the reputation of being wanderers, horse copers, metalworkers, and petty thieves. . . .

The Gypsies reached Spain via France in the 1400s and drifted slowly southward. It is claimed that there are earlier references to them in Andalusia, so the inference is that a wave of these migrants crossed North Africa before the northern branch reached Europe via the Balkans. But I have not found evidence of this. In Andalusia they tended to settle and cease their nomadic ways. Nowadays in the various regions you find names that are almost dynastic and suggest long settlement: the Amayas, Carmonas, and Heredias of Granada; and the Fernández, Vargas, and Ortega families in the Seville area. They have a much stronger sense of family than we do: second and even third cousins are part of the family. Could you even name your third cousins—that is to say, the descendants of your great-great-grand-father? When a Gypsy tells me that so-and-so is his cousin, I know only that they are related. So the word *clan* is appropriate.

The fact of settling and the possible arrival of Gypsy migrants via North Africa—these are not the only ways the Andalusian Gypsies (the Calós, as distinct from the Roma of elsewhere) differ from their northern cousins. There is a more important distinction. There can be no documentary evidence, except from biased documents of the law and the church, and so nothing can be proved. But there is a convincing theory that accounts for what would otherwise be baffling problems and mysteries.

It will be easier to explain if I state the problems first. The music of the Gypsies of different parts of the world has little in common other than the vitality of its rhythms, the fact that it lends itself to lively dance, and one or two formal traits that make the siguiriya, for example, identifiably Gypsy. Try putting this to the test by comparing a siguiriya with a Hungarian *czardas*, or the music of the Romanian Gypsies, such as that of the band Taraf de Haïdouks: they have nothing recognizable in common. The fact is, Gypsies adopted the music of the country they settled in and then colored it with their style. So what was the music these Gypsies found when they arrived in Andalusia? In the fifteenth century, Andalusia was inhabited in the hundreds of thousands by Moors, with a strong minority of Jews. Both had a long and strong tradition of music and poetry that made them noted even among their own peoples in the eastern Mediterranean. In 1492, at the end of the Reconquest of Spain by the Christians, the Jews were given the choice to abjure their God and convert to Christianity or else leave the country. An estimated 200,000 Jews converted, and the rest—perhaps as many again—went into exile and settled all round the Mediterranean, where they are known as Sephardim (from Sepharad, the Hebrew name for the Iberian peninsula). The same applied to the Moorish majority, though their expulsion was not final until a century later. Then most of them fled to Africa—and found themselves nowhere. They had been living in Spain for upward of eight hundred years, by which time they were a genetic mix of Arabs, Berbers, and many other peoples, mainly through marriage but also through the many *muwallads* (converts to Islam). When they reached the countries of the Mahgreb, they found they were considered outsiders in every sense, harshly treated and often enslaved. Large numbers returned in despair to Spain to live clandestinely. Meanwhile the converts who had stayed behind, Moorish or Jewish, were being so hounded by the Inquisition that many of them fled too. Literally, they took to the hills. And, in the tens or hundreds of thousands, these persecuted peoples disappeared—seemingly off the face of the earth. Two centuries and more later, when the Spanish Gypsies began to receive fairer treatment at the end of the eighteenth century and to emerge from the wilderness, they made up the greatest concentration of their kind in Europe. Today the estimates of their numbers vary between 200,000 and 700,000. When we remember that the Gypsies have long had a reputation of hospitality to fugitives, the mystery would seem to be solved . . .

Through those three hundred years from the sixteenth through the eighteenth centuries, the treatment these peoples suffered was not quite the same. The Gypsies were social outcasts, harried by the law, but not—officially— by the church. And, mainly, not for their race but for vagabondage. English statutes of the same period against "rogues and vagabonds" were no less harsh. In a way, the Gypsies brought it on themselves by refusing to conform to the laws and customs of the land they had settled in. They were marginalized, but largely because they chose to stick to their own chosen way of life. The civil law was neither so efficient nor so cruelly ruthless as the church, in the form of the Inquisition. With the exception of one dreadful period in the eighteenth century, when there was an attempt to enslave them all, a settled Gypsy plying a trade might pass unharmed; a Moor or a Jew could lose his life, painfully, merely for being one. So it would seem that over that long period—a shameful one for a so-called Christian society—the Jewish and Moorish peoples hid among the Gypsies, gradually merging with them. It wasn't hard: large areas of Spain were virtually unpopulated. I believe the Andalusian Gypsies as we know them today are the descendants of this ethnic blend.

This solution accounts for other problems, too, but this is not the place for detail, nor am I concerned to persuade others. My own conviction is reinforced by personal experience of the diversity of coloring and feature that I find among my Gypsy acquaintances. Some have clearly Negroid ancestry, some could play gods and goddesses in a Bollywood movie, while Isabel, my greengrocer from the heart of the Gypsy quarter of Jerez, could be typecast as a Jewish mother (see figures 29 and 30a–d). It may be relevant, too, that the Moors were cultivators, who brought the fertile soil of Anda-

Figure 29. Isabel, my greengrocer.

lusia to fruition. So far as I know, agriculture has never been a characteristic of Gypsy peoples outside Andalusia, yet the Gypsies of the Santiago district of Jerez have long been farmworkers. So I think the Calós, the Gypsies of Andalusia, are a rich ethnic and cultural mix of all the outcasts—Gypsy, Moor, and Jew.

Their language may throw some light on their origins, though in a negative way. George Borrow (1803–1881) was a prodigious linguist who learned Romany from English Gypsies in the days when they still used it. When he went to sell Bibles in Spain in the 1830s, he found that Romany had already been partly forgotten: the Calós were using the vocabulary, but within a Spanish syntax. If you speak Spanish, you will see this from the following verses, which he took down from their songs, and which you can also compare with the more recent lyrics I quote in chapter 5, in which the Gypsy component is less rich. I put in italics the words of the original that are in Caló. You will notice that even they have Spanish endings:

No *cameles* a *gachés*
por mucho que se *aromanen*
que al fin *ila* por partida
te *reverdisce* la *rati.*

Don't love outsiders
however pro-Gypsy
for that way you'll end up
with your blood spilled.

El *gate* de mi *trupo*
no se *muchobela* en *pani,*
se *muchobela* con la *rati*
de Juanito Ralí.

The shirt on my body
is not to be washed in water;
it's to be washed with the blood
of Juanito Ralí.

He *mangado* la *pani*
no me la *camelaron diñar*
he *chalado* a la *ulicha*
y me he *chibado* a *dustilar.*

I asked for water
they wouldn't give me any;
I went out to the street
and started to steal.

Por aquel *luchipen* abajo *abillela* un *balichoró* *abillela* a *goli goli*: *ustíla*me, *caloró*.	Down that hillside comes a pig, it comes a-squealing: take me, Gypsy.
La *puri* de *min dai* La *curaron* los *randes* Al *abillar* a la *Meligrana* Pa' *manguelarme metepé*.	My old mother was set upon by thieves on her way to Granada to plead for my release.
Ya están los *Calés balbales* cada uno en sus *querés* y *tosares* los pobrecitos los llevan al *jurepé*.	The rich Gypsies sit each in his own home, and all the poor ones get thrown in jail.

However rich the Moorish blood in their ancestry, you would not expect Arabic words to have entered the vocabulary, since the Moors' very lives depended on their being taken for Gypsies. By the same token, since such traces as remain of the Gypsy grammar show it to have been very complicated, it would not be surprising, with so many non-Gypsies among them, that the structure of the language deteriorated and was forgotten.

Today the Gypsy words that sprinkle the verses of songs are understood and used by all flamencos, both Gypsy and gachó. But among them are other words that the Gypsies themselves do not realize are not of their language. They are words of *germanía*—thieves' cant or prison slang. And commonest among these is *payo*, the very word usually thought to be the Caló for a non-Gypsy. I had spent months in Granada hearing the word used without any rude intent, simply as the normal word for one who is not a Caló. Then in Jerez, while in Gypsy company, I happened to refer to myself as a payo. The reaction was immediate: "Please don't say that. It's not a good word. You're not a payo, you're a gachó." I went to the library: *payo* started life as thieves' cant for a rustic booby, a mark easy to swindle. Perhaps the reason the Jerez Gypsies retained some awareness of its real sense was that they have been integrated for a long time and are respected members of society: they have no reason to treat the gachó as an enemy, whereas in most other areas of Andalusia they are suspected, sometimes even despised, and therefore alienated. Incidentally, Caló, their own word for a Gypsy, means "black"; the feminine is Calí, which takes you back to its Indian origins when you remember that Kali is the Hindu goddess of death, the destroyer. One can at least partly follow their wanderings by words picked up en route: the Caló for street is *ulicha,* and for road, *drom.* One is clearly the Russian *ulitza,* and the other the Greek *dromos.* (Indeed, both words are also used in this sense in Romanian.) Meanwhile, *gachó* is no less clearly the same as *gorgio,* the English Romany word for a non-Gypsy.

The tide began to turn (and flamenco music to emerge in public) after an edict of 1783 that, in effect, put the Gypsies back inside the pale of society. I have come across a verse of an old siguiriya that says, in effect, "the Gentlemen's sons held a party; three of us died that night." It sounds like a version of today's upper-class twits smashing up a restaurant: "Let's go and get a few Gypsies for a lark. Yoicks! Tallyho!" But it must have dated from before 1783.

By the 1830s the Gypsies of the towns were beginning to by joined by *gitanos bravíos*—"wild" Gypsies from the hills, and this seems the place to explain the word *flamenco.* Until recently it has been a mystery. The various theories were all of them pretty far-fetched. Above all, they were mere theories, unsupported by evidence. The word *flamenco* was said to derive from the Flemish courtiers who came to Spain with the Emperor Charles V five hundred years ago; or from the bird of the same name (flamingo); or from Gypsy soldiers who had given loyal service in the Flemish wars of the seventeenth century; or from the Arabic phrase *fellah mengu,* apparently meaning "peasant refugee." But then an Italian scholar, Mario Penna, set about the problem. He looked at a comment made by George Borrow in the 1830s,

Figure 30. Four Gypsy faces:
(a) the singer La Macarena;
(b) the retired dancer Agustín Monje;
(c) the retired dancer El Chiringuito;
(d) Rafael Fernández, who taught me Caló.

a

b

c

d

then looked for a historical basis for it—and found a convincing one. His explanation has only recently become more widely known with the translation of his book into Spanish. Borrow's comment was that the Gypsies were often called Flemings (*flamencos*) and had until recently also been called Germans. Borrow's phrase shows that the word *flamenco* refers to a nationality, not to courtiers or birds or whatever. The reason, as Mario Penna explains it, is this: for centuries the depopulation of Spain had been a problem, especially in Andalusia, where the expulsion of the Moors had left the land almost deserted. It was tackled in the eighteenth century under the enlightened monarch Carlos III. In 1767 a Bavarian adventurer calling himself Colonel Thürriegel was contracted by the government to supply six thousand worthy Catholic laborers and artisans from Germany and Flanders (*alemanes y flamencos*)—though, intriguingly, barbers were to be excluded. They were to be settled in the south, each with a small-holding, two cows, five sheep, and financial help until the first harvest. But the governments of the Germanic and Flemish states were unwilling to let the colonel recruit worthy citizens, so he produced six thousand riff-raff instead. These idlers and loafers soon left their bit of land and reverted to old habits of vagabondage, begging, and pilfering. Of all Spanish society, the peasants were traditionally the most anti-Gypsy (they, after all, had been the ones to lose the occasional pig or hen), and such folk were not expert ethnologists. So all wanderers of the roads came to be called *alemanes* or *flamencos*. And Borrow tells us that by the 1830s the term *German* had recently dropped from use. Thirty years later the word *flamenco* appears in print for the second time, but by now referring to the song, not the singer.

Today there are cultural traits that distinguish the Gypsies from those other peoples whose lands they inhabit, though not so strongly from other, non-Gypsy, Andalusians. These traits emerge more clearly in places where they remain more marginalized. In Granada, for example, I found that I virtually had to choose: associate either with Gypsies or with good (that is, non-

Gypsy) citizens. Going to live in Jerez was like a breath of fresh air: to be where people's racial consciousness shows only in their pride, and where in many cases I'm still not sure which of my acquaintances is Caló and which gachó, mainly because it never occurs to me to ask when it doesn't occur to them to tell me. But elsewhere it can be very different. You notice this partly because in some places, such as Seville and Granada, their communities have been destroyed. In Seville in the 1960s, the Gypsies were persuaded to sell their houses in the city's Triana district for what seemed to them good money, and they dispersed to the high-rise outskirts. Triana was cleaned up and became fashionable and yuppified. And then the Gypsies began to realize they had sold their souls as much as their houses. For Triana had been a tight-knit community as well as a sort of spiritual capital of Gypsydom. At about the same time in Granada, the Sacromonte, the traditional Gypsy quarter, where they lived in caves in the hillside, was declared unhealthy, and the Gypsies were rehoused. Their community, too, was dispersed among the high-rise blocks of the outskirts. Today there are no zambras in Granada. Instead, there is a social problem.

There is no such problem among the flamencos, however—the community of those who live by it as performers or who simply live to enjoy the art, whether Gypsy or gachó. These are good people to know—friendly, helpful, and of a patrician courtesy. Indeed, in the areas such as Granada where Gypsies are marginalized, they seem more traditional, as though of an earlier generation than the ones I was later to know in western Andalusia. Throughout Andalusia, at all levels of society, hospitality is important enough for it to be unthinkable not to offer a drink to any visitor, invited or not. A small matter, you may think, and one that applies to us all—but the first time a Granada Gypsy invited me into his home, he said with intense formality, standing before me after I had sat down: "Robin, my house is your house, and everything in it." Thereupon he invited me to have a drink. We were on easygoing terms, it was a Sunday morning not long after breakfast, and the last thing I wanted was a beer or a whisky (the standard drinks among the flamenco community there). But the formal speech alerted me, so I accepted. He unsealed a bottle of expensive brandy, poured out one glassful (none for himself), and presented it to me, just as formally. To him, hospitality was a matter of ritual importance.

The Gypsy work philosophy may well be the same all over Andalusia, but it is, again, more noticeable in areas of greater marginalization. Making money is considered dandy—indeed, you come across some fairly startling rapacity in the fees asked by some singers. But not money-making that involves enslavement to a daily grind. The taranta, for instance, could not be Gypsy in origin, for it is unthinkable that a Gypsy should *choose* to take a job that condemned him to daylong labor in the dark. In the sixteenth and seventeenth centuries, they had been sometimes enslaved in the mines of western Andalusia, and there was one instance in 1745, but not a century later when the *taranta* evolved. More important than money is the freedom that gives you the choice to work or not, according to mood or need. *Yo mando en mi hambre*, said El Chocolate: "I am the master of my own hunger." This emerges less clearly in a town of long settlement and integration such as Jerez, where I count a lawyer, a television producer, and a business manager among the Gypsies I have met. But then it is also a town where only two of the beggars are Gypsy—and they are both simple. With this non-work ethic goes a tendency not to plan for the future ("Take no heed for the morrow"— they have a respectable precedent). One friend told me that she had been determined not to marry a fellow Gypsy because she wanted a man who would give their children a better life.

Perhaps the most marked of the Gypsy cultural traits concerns the importance of the family, and by extension, of the community. The damage done to Triana, in Seville, and the Sacromonte, in Granada, lay in the dispersal of its community, one in which the elders are always cared for and respected, but above all, consulted and listened to. In their own language:

Who Are the Gypsies of Andalusia?

Rebliná ur puró	Respect for the old
sina a lirí	is the law
enré ler calós	among the Gypsies.

Among a people for whom the police have been the traditional enemy, a close community is important for keeping order, for the elders sitting at their doorsteps can see what the young are up to and keep them in check. The Gypsies are shocked that we put our old folk into homes. They, too, have single-parent families, or ones where both parents have to go out to work, but thanks to their extended sense of family, there is always someone to look after those who need it, young or old. And if there is no family, the neighbors cope.

In eastern Andalusia, at least, the traditional Gypsy wedding still sometimes happens. My knowledge is second-hand, and comes in one instance from a gachó who recorded some of it (not all, because both battery and his stamina ran out before the three days and nights were over), and in another from a Gypsy who was married at fifteen and divorced at twenty-five and told me something of both procedures. On the wedding day, all but the two families leave while the mataora tests the girl's virginity. When she comes out and exhibits the red-stained handkerchief, the celebration takes off, and they sing and dance the alboreá. How widespread this custom is I have not felt it pertinent to ask. By contrast, in my own town, where there is no marginalization, I was one of a dozen gachés among about two hundred guests at a party celebrating an engagement. The family was there in force, including the older generation. When I photographed my host, he insisted on picking up and holding a toddler. I put his behavior down to the Andalusians' love for children. Not so: it was his own. He and the mother had decided to get married. This may be commonplace today, yet only a generation or two ago the girl might have been killed for dishonoring her family, for losing her *lachi dor drupo* (bodily purity). And in some parts of Andalusia she would be in trouble even today.

Chapter 7

In this strongly clan-centered society, the mother is dominant and is given a love that borders on reverence—though not always by the daughter-in-law:

Tu madre no dice ná	Your mother says nothing
Tu madre es de las que muerden	your mother is one of those who bite
Con la boca cerrá.	with her mouth shut.

But among the menfolk, even today she is revered. A friend of mine called Bernard the Moorslayer disappeared from the clubs he frequented. His mother had died and he went into strict mourning, shutting himself away from social life for an entire year.

His name is not so startling as you might think. It is characteristic of the Calós to acquire a nickname (*apodo* or *mote*) that takes over, sometimes to the point where their surnames are known only to the Civil Registry. El Bizco de los Camarones (The Cross-Eyed Shrimp Seller) is so named even on the CDs he has produced. One of the men who taught me Caló, Rafael Fernández, uses his real name, perhaps because he works for the city hall, but in his own quarter, among his own family and friends, he is called only Nene (Baby), an apodo given to him by jeering classmates when he was fourteen because he wanted to study. El Bizco's apodo is an accurate description. Others are less obvious: the Granadan singer Antonio el Colorao (Tony the Red) has black hair. But his eldest brother had sandy-red hair, a rarity among Gypsies, so he became El Colorao—and all his siblings after him. The famous Camarón (The Shrimp) was so dubbed as a pallid child by the great Caracol (The Snail)—who already had his own apodo at the age of twelve, when he won a prize at de Falla's 1922 cante jondo competition.

I don't want to leave the subject without mention of the Gypsies' strong sense of tragic destiny. Their refusal to conform to the norms of the countries they passed through is enough to explain their persecution. But why should the human mind associate tragic destiny with nomadism in itself? Why the concept of being *condemned* to wander? Why the Flying Dutchman, the Wandering Jew, Cain? This is not the place to expand on the matter. Here it is enough to say that the Gypsy, though long settled now, is more aware of tragic destiny than the rest of us.

This brief sketch has no pretension to be more than an introduction, but one that I felt necessary because of the Gypsies' key role in flamenco. It is not exclusive to them. But they are its principal torchbearers, and always have been. Their own opinions range from dogged belief that flamenco is theirs alone to the more widespread opinion neatly summed up by the dancer Manuela Carrasco. When asked what was the difference between Gypsy and non-Gypsy flamenco, she said: "None at all" and added, with a smile: "but then again we Gypsies do have a quality all our own."

Appendix 1

GLOSSARY

This glossary has two parts: first, flamenco terms, and second, Gypsy words that commonly appear in flamenco songs.

Flamenco terms

aflamencao—flamencoized; folk songs sung by flamencos are referred to as *aflamencao*.

a golpe—sung to the rhythm of only a stick, or knuckles on the table. It is considered the purest form of flamenco. The singer uses knuckle and fingernails. If you see a man with a thick callus on the back of his middle finger and a nail bruised black, he sings *a golpe*.

alboreá—song form; see p. 102.

alegrías—song form; see p. 111.

alzapúa—guitar-playing technique that uses the back of the thumbnail.

angel—see *duende*.

a palo seco—with no accompaniment; originally a nautical term meaning "under bare poles"—that is, with no sails.

apodo—nickname such as many Gypsies acquire for life; see also *mote*.

a seco—playing the guitar *rasgueado*, with the fingers of the left hand damping the strings.

atravesarse—for the guitarist, to cut corners and rhythm during a *falseta*, making the dancer's job difficult.

babeo—repeated meaningless sounds such as *bababa* in the middle of words. See also *glosolalias* and *vibratos*.

bailaor, -ora—flamenco dancer, as opposed to *bailarín*, which is any other dancer. The line is often crossed: Antonio Gades was a *bailarín* who could dance good flamenco; Cristina Hoyos is a pure *bailaora* who can use all the techniques of the *bailarín*.

baile—flamenco dance; other forms are referred to as *danza*.

baile del mantón—a dance with a shawl.

balanceo y vaivén—swaying of the body and hips. *Balanceo* is gentle; *vaivén* is violent.

bamberas—song form; see p. 152.

bata de cola—dress with a train.

bonito—"pretty"; in other words, not good flamenco.

braceo—the dancer's use of the arms.

bulerías—song form; see p. 104.

bullanguero—festive; adjectival form of of *bulerías*.

cabal—the final verse of a *siguiriya*; literally, honest, exact, complete. The way of ending a song is important and has other words to describe it (see *remate*). Most are ended by speeding up; this is true of the *siguiriya* too, but the *cabal* is often in the major key.

cambio—change of key and lightening of tone to end a song.

campanilleras—song form; see p. 152.

cantaor, -ora—flamenco singer; any other kind of singer is called a *cantante*.

cante—flamenco song; any other sort is *canto*. See also *a palo seco* and *toque*.

cante chico—literally, "little song"; includes festive forms such as the *alegrías* and *tango*.

cante grande—the major forms of deep song, such as the *toná, martinete, siguiriya, soleá,* and *carcelera*. Formerly known as *cante jondo*.

cante intermedio—varies (that is, between *cante chico* and *cante grande*) according to who is singing it—and who is saying it.

cante pa' alante—literally, "singing from in front"; singing not done for dancers, with the singer seated.

cante pa' atrás—literally, "singing from behind"; singing for dancers, with the singer standing.

cantes de ida y vuelta—songs brought back from Latin America.

cantes de levante—songs from the eastern provinces of Granada, Jaen, Almería, and Murcia.

cantiñas—song form; see p. 111.

caracoles—song form; see p. 113.

cartageneras—song form; see p. 138.

castañuelas—castanets; see also *palillos*.

cejillo—capodaster or capo, used by guitarists.

chasquidos—see pitos.

chufla—any festive and frivolous song.

cierre—close of a series of steps or a line of song; some dancers use it to mean *desplante*.

colombianas—song form; see p. 145.

compás—a measure or bar; flamencos use the word to mean both (a) the twelve-count and (b) the rhythmic skill of a performer.

contratiempo—cross-rhythms, including syncopation and rubato.

convulsión—see *torsión y convulsion*.

copla—verse of (flamenco) *cante*, as against the *cuplé* of (non-flamenco) *canto*. It may have three, four, or five lines.

corrido—ballad, nowadays called *romance*.

corte—the way the singer ends a musical phrase; see also *dejes*.

crótalo—Phoenician and Roman form of castanets; it had a handle and had to be played with both hands. The poet Martial refers to them as *crusmata baetica* (coming from southern Spain).

cuadro—a flamenco troupe.

cuplé—see *copla*.

debla—a form of the *toná*. It is old song form, now seldom used.

dejes—the way the singer ends a phrase; the cadence; see also *corte*.

desgarro—literally, "tear, rip"; wildness, heartbreak.

desplante—technically, a point in the dance that marks the end of a section. In fact, a high point, a climax, in the dance at which the dancer pauses and the audience applauds.

diapasón—the neck or fingerboard of the guitar.

duende—literally, "spirit" or "demon"; it suggests possession. The word is bandied about too much, often in reverential tones that to my mind form part of the damaging pseudery that surrounds flamenco. Every performance art in the world has moments that make the audience hold its breath. Flamencos tend to prefer the word *angel.* The best definition of *duende* that I have heard is: "duende is a ten-year-old singing all the tragic experience of his forebears. . . . Every good singer is dipping into the well of flamenco."

escobilla—literally, "broom"; the section of the dance in which the dancer does an extended *zapateado.* This is also the term for the shuffle you see in some South American dances, so the term may be an Americanism.

escuela bolera—a graceful and balletic form of the old bolero; dance in 3/4 time popular in the last century. It is still taught by, among others, Matilde Coral in Triana.

falsetas—solo passages on the guitar at start and between verses of the song; sometimes called *variaciones.*

fandangos—a family of song forms; see p. 121.

faralá, faralaes—Andalusian dress worn at festivals; because of its weight, it is not worn by flamenco dancers; literally, "frill [attached to a dress]"; by extension, flashy, in vulgar taste.

farruca—song form; see p. 139.

figura—a star; a performer who has achieved name and fame.

gancho—literally, "hook"; by extension, anything that gets to you, that "hooks" you (*tiene ~*).

garra—literally, "claws"; guts, force

garrotín—song form; see p. 141.

gesto—facial expression; in other contexts it also means "gesture."

glosolalias—meaningless sounds (such as *tiriti tran tran tran*) used in the song; see also *babeo.*

golpe—tapping the face of the guitar with the second and/or third finger while playing.

granaína—song form; see p. 131.

guajira—song form; see p. 143.

jaberas—song form; see p. 127.

jalear—to encourage with words and/or *palmas*.

jaleo—the vocal encouragement given to performers when the audience calls out such phrases as *ezo!, ezoé!, arsa!, olé!, que sabe!, toma!,* and *toma que te toma!*

jipío—a cry (such as *ay*) used by the singer to find his pitch or to put into the middle of a song; also called *quejío*.

jondo—the Gypsy pronunciation of *hondo* (deep); formerly applied to the song forms but nowadays used more to describe a manner of singing.

juerga—a get-together of flamencos among themselves, usually with only *cante a golpe*. Also may mean a lively party. The word may be the Gypsy pronunciation of *huelga* (leisure).

ligado—in guitar, sounding the note with the fingers of the left hand only.

llamada—literally, "call"; the opening of a dance; it may be a movement forward with the feet, together with raising and lowering of arms.

macho—usually a three-line verse used as a *remate* (see below) to the *siguiriya*; it is generally in a major key.

malagueñas—song form; see p. 126.

martinetes—song form; see p. 86.

media granaína—song form; see p. 131.

melisma—series of notes sung on one syllable; also called *gorjeo* (warbling) and sometimes *modulaciones.* It is the part of the song that, to ears unaccustomed to it, may sound like unmusical wailing.

milonga—song form; see p. 145.

mineras—song form; see p. 138.

mirabras—song form; see p. 114.

mote—see *apodo.*

mudanza—see *punteado.*

murcianas—song form; see p. 139.

nanas—song form; see p. 153.

oposición—refers to the essential asymmetry of flamenco; in other words, if the arms are going one way the face will look the other. Flamenco abhors symmetry, so the principle of *oposición* is the nearest thing in flamenco to a law.

palillos—flamenco name for castanets.

palmas—clapping. It is an art, requiring skill and knowledge of *compás*; while others mark the *compás*, a good *palmero* can play variations on it with surprising effect and effectiveness.

palmas altas—percussive effect performed with the fingers of the right hand on the left palm, resulting in a sharp sound.

palmas sordas—muted clapping done with cupped hands (usually by the singer).

palmero—performer of *palmas*.

palo—song form; literally, a suit at cards. They fall into two main categories: those done in free rhythm (*sin compás*), which include the *toná* (see p. 86); *martinete* (p. 86); *carcelera* (p. 87); *fandangos* (*grandes* or *personales*) (p. 128); *malagueña* (p. 126); *jabera* (p. 127); *granaína* [p. 131], and *cantes de Levante* (*cartagenera* [p. 138], *taranta* [p. 136], and *minera* [p. 138]); and those done in rhythm (*con compás*), which include the *seguiriya* (p. 89); *serrana* (p. 96); *liviana* (p. 94); *petenera* (p. 117); *soleá* (p. 97); *caña* (p. 116); *polo* (p. 116); *alboreá* (p. 102); *bulería* (p. 104); *cantiñas* (*alegrías* [p. 111], *mirabrás* [p. 114], *caracoles* [p. 113]); *tiento* (p. 107); *tango* (p. 107); *taranto* (p. 138); most *fandangos* (p. 121) (including the *rondeña* [p. 125]); *farruca* (p. 139); *garrotín* (p. 141); and all *cantes de ida y vuelta* (*guajira* [p. 143], *milonga* [p. 145], *colombiana* [p. 145], and *rumba* [p. 145]). A complete listing is given in chapter 5.

palo seco—see *a palo seco*.

paso—step or series of steps (as in the *paso de tango*).

paso lateral—sideways movement.

payo—commonly thought to be the Gypsy word for a non-Gypsy, but in fact prison slang for an easy mark, a sucker. The Caló word for non-Gypsy is *gachó* (pl. *gachés*).

pellizco—literally, "nip, pinch"; that quality (usually in a dancer) that turns you on. The first of a hierarchy of expressions that goes through *puntas de velo* (which we would call goosepimples, but literally referring to the hair on your arms standing up), to *angel*, to *duende* (see above).

peña—flamenco club; in the strongly flamenco towns along the Seville-Cádiz axis, they tend to be welcoming and to be the best possible place to hear and see good things; they are also the nearest equivalent of the English pub. In other areas, some are so exclusive they have a guard on the door to keep out non-members, and even the performers are made to feel like servants allowed into the drawing room at Christmas. Thirty yards down the street from one such (the Platería) in Granada is an anonymous door to a place owned by a Gypsy singer where the real flamencos congregate. Every small town, village, or suburb is likely to have its own *peña*. Here, to continue the parallel, there is definitely no saloon bar. Locals come for a drink or a game of dominoes, and when the soccer game is over, the television is switched off and people perform—sometimes locals, sometimes invited *figuras* (see above).

peteneras—song form; see p. 117.

picar—on guitar, to pluck, as against *rasguear* (see *rasqueado*); see also *pulsar*.

pitos—finger snapping; also called *chasquidos*.

playero—lamenting: a *playera* is an old name for the *siguiriya*.

por arriba—on guitar, in the hand position for the key of E (or raised from there with the capo).

por medio—on guitar, in the hand position for the key of A (or raised from there with the capo).

pregones—street vendor's chant.

pulsar—see *picar*.

punteado—steps and movements that are not part of the *zapateado*. It subdivides into *paseo* (a walking movement) and *mudanzas* (more complicated steps; literally, "variations").

puntear—see *picar*.

quejío—see *jipío*.

rajo—see *voz afillá*.

rasgueado—on guitar, a drumroll effect created by using the backs of the fingers—that is, the nails—one after another.

remate—way of ending a song, either by raising the pitch, changing to the major, or simply speeding up. See also *cambio* and *cabal*.

roás—Sacromonte form of the *alboreá*.

romances—song form; see p. 88.

romeras—song form; see p. 114.

rondeñas—song form; see p. 125.

rumbas—song form; see p. 145.

Sacromonte—a hillside in Granada riddled with cave dwellings, in which the Gypsies used to live. It was one of the heartlands of Gypsy flamenco, with a style all its own. After flooding one winter in the 1960s the Gypsies were, for health reasons, resettled in the suburbs, a move that destroyed their community. Some of the caves are maintained for flamenco performances. Higher up the hill, on the Albaicín side, many of the houses still lead back into caves.

saeta—song form; see p. 148.

sevillanas—song form; see p. 151.

sevillanas boleras—see *escuela bolera.*

siguiriyas—song form; see p. 89.

soleá por bulería—song form; see p. 103.

soleares—song form; see p. 97.

son—all sound accompanying the flamenco song (guitar, clapping, finger snapping, knuckle tapping).

sonanta—flamenco slang for guitar.

soniquete—literally, "droning"; it is applied to performers being what jazz players call "in the groove."

tablao—the venue for a tourist-oriented flamenco show.

tablas—literally, "boards"; the stage on which the dance is performed; *tiene tablas* means "to be [an] experienced [performer]."

tangos—song form; see p. 107.

tanguillos—song form; see p. 110.

tapa—the face of the guitar.

tarantas—song form; see p. 136.

tarantos—song form; see p. 138.

templar—to tune.

temple—tuning or temperament; in the song, it means the *quejíos* and *jipíos* and humming of the singer so as to find his tone and pitch., while guitarist is playing his initial *falsetas.*

temporeras—song form; see p. 153.

tercio—section (phrase, sentence, line); a line of verse; a musical phrase (literally, "third").

tientos—song form; see p. 107.

tocaor—guitarist.

tonás—song form; see p. 86.

toque—guitar playing.

torsión y convulsión—stages, usually in the *soleá*, wherein the dancer reaches a more or less ecstatic state; her body twists and writhes (which is the literal meaning of these words) and her head may jerk from side to side. When Charo Espino danced one of the best *soleares* I have seen, for Paco Peña's company in London in 1997, the *Times* critic dismissed it as cold because "unspontaneous"—one of the most inept criticisms I have come across. Few dancers alive manage a *soleá* that grows as naturally and organically to a climax of *torsiones* as Charo's did.

tremolo—on guitar, playing a bass note with thumb and high (melody) notes with fingers in quick succession to make a continuous sound. Classical guitar plays four notes with thumb, ring finder, middle finger, and index finger; flamenco plays five notes with thumb, index finger, ring finger, middle finger, and index finger. It is of course more complicated than this; I refer guitarists to Paco Peña's description (see bibliography).

Triana—the traditional Gypsy quarter of Seville, now yuppified.

trilla, cantes de—song form; see p. 153.

vaivén—see *balanceo y vaivén*.

verdiales—song form; see p. 123.

vibrato—repeated meaningless sounds uttered during the song, such as *jajaja*, but, unlike *babeo*, not within a word.

villancicos—song form; see p. 149.

vito—Andalusian folk song and dance in fast 3/8 time (not flamenco).

voz afillá—hoarse voice like that of El Fillo, a nineteenth-century singer; this quality is also known as *rajo*.

zambra—(i) a form of Sacromonte *tango*; (ii) a noisy fiesta originally of the Moors (from the Arabic word meaning either a flute or musicians). In the Sacromonte (Granada) it means a kind of performance that you are likely to hear in the caves, mostly upbeat, in 2/4 time. It may be based on the Gypsy wedding. Thus the dances include the *cachucha* and the *mosca*, which are mimic dances: the *cachucha* plays out in dance form the bridegroom apologizing for deflowering the bride; the *mosca* is danced by four women who imitate the action of brushing away flies. It was revived in the third Cumbre Flamenca in Madrid.

zapateo, zapateado—the form of tap dancing peculiar to flamenco. One of its central characteristics (which it shares with jazz) is variations on a rhythmic theme, the imaginative creation of cross- and counterrhythms made by hitting the floor with various parts of the foot and with various effects. They include *planta* (stamp with the whole foot; also known as *golpe*); *media-planta* (stamp with the sole only); *flas* (flash; scrape with the sole; also called *resbalo*); *punta* or *puntera* (with the toe cap); and *tacón* (with the heel).

zarongo—see *zorongo*.

zorongo—an old song and dance in 2/4 time (not flamenco), revived by Federico García Lorca; also called *zarongo*.

Common Gypsy words used in the songs

acais—eyes.
bata—mother; see also *dai*.
Caló (*fem.* **Calí**)—Gypsy; Gypsy language.
calorró—Gypsy (adj.).
camelar—to want, to love.
chalar—to go.
chaval—lad, boy.
chavalillo—kid, small boy.
chorreles—children.
chungo, -a—ugly, bad.
churumbel—boy.

cuco—pudendum; in Spanish it means "cute."

dai—see *bata*.

debel—see *devé*.

debla—see *devé*; see also the glossary of flamenco terms.

debla barea—meaning is unknown. "Great goddess," "I can't go on," and "[cante] de Blas Barea" (or "de Bla' Barea") have all been suggested. Each fits some songs but makes no sense in others. The *debla* is also a song form.

devé—God.

diñar—to give.

diquelar—to see.

ducas—troubles (from *duco*, "spirit").

duquelas—see *ducas*.

endiñar—to give violently, for example a punch.

gachó (*fem.* **gachí**; *pl.* **gachés**)—non-Gypsy.

gerá (*pl.* **gerais**)—(non-Gypsy) gentleman.

jerá—see *gerá*.

juncal—graceful, beautiful (Jerezano Gypsies sometimes say *jucal*).

lachí—shy, shame-faced, modest.

marelar—to kill.

mar(r)ar—see *marelar*.

naquerar—to talk.

parné—money.

pinrés—legs.

undebel—see *devé*.

Appendix 2

CARLOS SAURA'S *FLAMENCO*

After the success of his flamenco versions of *Carmen*, Manuel de Falla's ballet *El amor brujo*, Federico García Lorca's *Bodas de sangre*, and his documentary *Sevillanas*, Carlos Saura made a documentary entitled simply *Flamenco*. It was disappointing. He invited a brilliant cast but kept to his formula of filming in a massive studio (in this case a disused Seville railway station) divided into cubicles: he did not realize the importance to flamencos of atmosphere. He was asking them to do their thing in clinical surroundings, without audience, without *jaleo*. They tried. But it just doesn't work well that way. For example, the film starts with a *bulería* danced, among others, by the fourteen-year-old Manuela Nuñez. When she was nine she did a bulería that set the house alight: she is a born performer, with an expressive little monkey face that lights up when in the presence of an audience. They love it, she sparkles still more, and the whole thing takes off. Here it was dead. She tried—too hard—to put it on for a camera; she forced it, and knew it, and her dance did not come to life. But the video is easily obtainable, and it does give you the chance to familiarize yourself with the song and dance. Some of it is good, though much is atypical: many of the performers seem to have decided that for a film they should invent and do things differently. In what follows I give a commentary on the items—minimal where it has already been discussed in chapter 5, or where I don't think the item helpful.

1. *Bulerías*. See above; yet these are all fine performers.
2. *Guajira*. See chapter 5. Merché Esmeralda, of the old, graceful school, does it well.
3. *"Alegrías" as guitar variations*. Actually, these are more accurately called cantiñas

—Manolo Sanlucar doesn't touch the tune of the alegrías. For that, item 17 is more helpful.

4. *Farruca*. Not a useful introduction. Joaquín Cortés is a showman first and last. See chapter 5.

5. *Martinete*. Manuel Moneo is good. Manuel Agujetas is magnificent.

6. *Danced martinete*. Mario Maya makes it a flamenco ballet, sketching a story. He is a fine dancer; but this shows why many flamencos accuse him of being a bailarín rather than a bailaor. Of the two young men with him, Diego Llori has since become a *figura*.

7. *Fandangos de Huelva*. This one comes from the village of Alosno. Well performed. The second solo singer is Paco Toronjo, who was one of a pair of brothers (the other has died) largely responsible for popularizing it among flamencos. Its folk-song characteristics are evident: it is sung in chorus and has a set tune and a refrain .

8. *Soleá 1*. Fernanda was one of the great singers in her day and is now very old, so her soleá is short and restrained. Nonetheless, some of the character that made her so well loved comes through.

9. *Peteneras*. The peteneras are a form in rhythm. As he goes along, José Menese sings it more and more in free rhythm. This makes it hard to impossible for the dancer to move to it. Luckily we only see fragments of María Pagés coping. The singer treats the tune more freely than usual, too. Altogether not very helpful.

10. *Siguiriya*. Morente's siguiriyas are certainly not a model—more an experimental departure. The same applies to his guitarist. Deep down, they have the siguiriya compás, but it is all but unrecognizable.

11. *Soleá 2, danced*. Some consider Manuela Carrasco the finest dancer alive. Her dancing is idiosyncratic and very Gypsy. Here she is supported by José Mercé and Moraíto, both among the best. All three here treat the soleá too idiosyncratically to help you much.

12. *Soleá 3, danced*. This is the one most likely to help you. Another quintessentially Gypsy performance. El Farruco, who died recently, was self-taught but instructed and launched his grandson Farruquito (see chapter 3). Chocolate is

a star singer who shows in this video that his nickname came from his complexion, not habits (*chocolate* also means marijuana).

13. *Taranta.* Carmen Linares is the obvious choice for a taranta, which comes from her hometown. This performance complements my CD illustration. She seems to like virtuoso guitarists such as Rafael Riqueni, whose playing is too *bonito* for this song. Compare this with El Coquillo's playing on my CD.

14. *Tangos.* These are good: true flamenco, true Gypsy. There is no tiento here, with its characteristic tune. But these three give you a guided tour round the tangos. Between them and Paco de Lucía's rather jazzy version (see no. 18), you should become familiar with the two types of tune: the first comes down the scale four steps at a time, which is perhaps clearest in the guitar version; the second is sung clearly by Aurora Vargas and goes up the scale (to a B-flat), then dips a bit, and then does it again a tone higher.

15. *Villancico.* This is folk, not flamenco, but it is done by flamencos. These are people from the peña Tío José de Paula in the Barrio Santiago, one of the Gypsy quarters in Jerez. They do it as they do every Christmas at a *zambomba* (Christmas caroling party round a bonfire). Ignore the unfortunate lighting on Tomasa la Macanita's nose: you can hear the gorgeous voice that makes her so much loved.

16. Lole and Manuel are too much themselves to be classified. They have their roots in flamenco but make a popular music whose appeal ranges far beyond Andalusia. This song, "La mariposa," is based on the compás of the bulería, which, together with the tango rhythm, accounts for nearly all their songs.

17. *Alegrías 2.* Danced in the bata de cola in the old bolero style, which is balletic, not flamenco. But the singers are both from Cádiz and among the best for the alegrías. Rancapino's is a model for the song; Chano Lobato sings a variation on the tune. Matilde Coral's dance is more flamenco than her pupils'.

18. *Tangos.* These are done with a jazz touch. Paco de Lucía's playing ranges from classical concerto to the purest flamenco, via jazz and much else.

19. *"Modern" bulerías, as far as the song goes.* Tomatito plays more traditionally (he partnered the legendary singer Camarón). The dancers, too, are pure flamenco: Belén Maya is Mario's daughter, and her arm movements are all her

own. Joaquín Grilo has since this film developed into one of the finest dancers.

20. *Rumbas.* These are pop fusion.

The film, with rather heavy-handed symbolism, opens out onto a crowd of youths moving to a *soleá* rhythm and on to the railway station with street noises. We are to understand that flamenco's future is flourishing and in good hands.

Appendix 3

BIBLIOGRAPHY

Books

On flamenco

Blas Vega, José, and Manuel Ríos Ruiz. *Diccionario enciclopédico ilustrado del flamenco*. 2 vols. Madrid: Editorial Cinterco, 1988, 1990. In Spanish.

> A massive work of scholarship. The flamencologist's bible.

Gamboa, José Manuel, and Pedro Calvo, *Guía libre del flamenco*. Madrid: Sociedad General de Autores y Editores, 2001. In Spanish.

> I haven't seen this book. Gamboa is knowledgeable, and the book sets out to give details on flamencos and flamenco clubs and venues, which should make it an excellent companion to anyone looking for the real thing. At 450 pages, it is hardly a pocket book, but it may be useful.

Howson, Gerald. *The Flamencos of Cádiz Bay*. Rev. ed. Westport, Conn.: Bold Strummer, 1994.

> First published nearly forty years ago, and things have changed—but it is still a good read.

Penna, Mario. *El flamenco y los flamencos: Historia de los gitanos españoles y su música*. Seville: Portada Editorial, 1996. In Spanish.

> On everything that thoughtful scholarship can produce, this is a fine book. His conclusions sometimes go wrong because his knowledge is theoretical: he has listened to and watched flamencos but not known them or Andalusia personally.

Pohren, Donn. *The Art of Flamenco*. Madrid: Society of Spanish Studies, 1962.

> Written in 1962, this is the first and perhaps the only book that sets out to explain flamenco. It is a classic, though it predates CDs so that I did not find

it greatly helpful in identifying the song forms and therefore decided to write my own.

———. *Lives and Legends of Flamenco*. Madrid: Society of Spanish Studies, 1988.

A biographical dictionary. If you read Spanish, Gamboa's book may be more useful.

———. *A Way of Life*. Madrid: Society of Spanish Studies, 1979.

The third book in Pohren's trilogy.

Schreiner, Claus, ed. *Flamenco: Gypsy Dance and Music from Andalusia*. Portland, Ore.: Amadeus Press, 1990.

The experience of a group of Germans studying song, dance, and guitar in Andalusia. It is good on their own experience, but needs the caveat that they are often wrong on anything learned at second hand: they seem unaware of the ferocious local chauvinism of the Andalusian and tend to accept whatever they are told.

Stimpson, Michael, ed. *The Guitar: A Guide for Students and Teachers*. Oxford and New York: Oxford University Press, 1988.

Chapter 13, by Paco Peña, is the best introduction to flamenco of any sort—not just for guitarists. First-hand knowledge of flamenco and of music; all fact, no flim-flam.

Woodall, James. *In Search of the Firedance*. London: Sinclair-Stevenson, London, 1992.

An attempt to relate flamenco to recent Spanish history. He has admirable knowledge of flamenco but is no historian and tends to accept what he is told.

On the Gypsies

Borrow, George Henry. *The Bible in Spain, or, The Journeys, Adventures, and Imprisonments of an Englishman in an Attempt to Circulate the Scriptures in the Peninsula*. Many editions.

———. *The Zincali: An Account of the Gypsies of Spain with an Original Collection of Their Songs and Poetry*. Many editions.

Writing in the 1840s, Borrow had knowledge of the Gypsies and acquaintance with them and their language that was—and remains—unrivaled.

Fonseca, Isabel. *Bury Me Standing: The Gypsies and Their Journey.* New York: Vintage, 1996.

The best book on Gypsies, though not the Andalusian Calós. A good read, yet thoroughly researched. The information it contains you can trust, in a way you can trust very little of the work written by most ethnologists. It is not just that she writes from experience, but that she has the wit to see that asking Gypsies questions is *not* the way to find the truth. She is almost unique in that, while she clearly likes them, she never sentimentalizes or lets her liking distort her judgment. I am constantly amazed that so many ethnologists romanticize the gypsies. I had the luxury of time and decided never to ask them questions, but to just wait till they accepted me (or not) and pick up what came my way.

Luna, José Carlos de. *Los Gitanos de la Bética.* Cádiz: University of Cádiz, 1989. Facsimile edition, in Spanish.

First-hand knowledge.

Videos

Saura, Carlos. *Flamenco.* New York: New Yorker Video, 1995, 1998. See Appendix 2.

Saura, Carlos. *Sevillanas.* Los Angeles: Mirada Video, 1992, 1996.

Sevillanas are not flamenco, but this is a brilliant film, in contrast to the rather flat *Flamenco*. There are also videos of Saura's versions of Federico García Lorca's *Bodas de sangre* (Los Angeles: Voyager, 1981); *Carmen* (Los Angeles: Media Home Entertainment, 1984, 1986); and Manuel de Falla's *El amor brujo* (Beverly Hills: Pacific Arts Video, 1987).

Among teaching videos, the La Luz series is the most widespread and quite good (Videos Flamencos de la luz, distributed in North America by Alegrias Productions). The Poal Productions series I don't recommend: it covers most dance forms but there is very little example and much glorifying of the dancer.

Gitanos de Jerez produces a double video for the soleá and the seguiriya that deserves notice: in contrast to the Poal film, there is a *brief* introduction. Thereafter there is no commentary at all. But you see each form no fewer than six times—all slightly slower than in real life. First, Irene Carrasco shows the woman's version of the soleá, once with the camera concentrating on the upper body (but in split screen so that you can always look at the whole person), then concentrating on the footwork, and finally in full view. Then Juan Antonio Tejero does the same for the man's version. Then they do the same again for the siguiriya. If you are a serious dance student, I think this is the best. Manuel Morao and Gitanos de Jerez, *Soleá y seguiriya* (1999). Apartado 592, 11480 Jerez de la Frontera, (Cádiz), Spain.

For aspiring guitarists, Encuentro Productions has an excellent series of teaching videos, of which the one by Merengue of Córdoba is perhaps the best for learning. Dorfstrasse 71, CH-8706 Meilen, Switzerland. www.encuentro.ch.

Agujetas Cantaor, the 1998 documentary by Dominique Abel (Golden Spice Award, San Francisco, 2000), is available on videocassette from www.flamencoworld.com. On it you can hear the singing of Manuel Agujetas, one the most powerful flamencos of all time. He is a phenomenon. The soundtrack is also available on compact disc.

Compact discs

Compact discs have come out by the hundreds, and any list must be personal, highly selective, and arbitrary. So I shall recommend singers, rather than their discs, leaving it to you to pick up what you can find. But one must mention the magisterial *Magna antología del cante flamenco* (Madrid: Hispavox), which comes in ten CDs, boxed, with a booklet by the director José Blas Vega. The collection is historical, originally published in 1955, cleaned up from old 78 rpm recordings. It contributed to the revival of flamenco by showing the younger generation how their predecessors did it—singers whose memory was revered but whose singing had not been available.

If you want the singers of the past, the company Sonifolk has put on CD the recordings of such singers as Niña de los Peines (1890–1969) and Manuel Torre (1890–1969, recorded 1909–30). They call him Torres, but Torre (tower) was his nickname. See sonifolk@sonifolk.com.

Singers

Anything you hear from any of the older generation still performing—Manuel Agujetas, Chocolate, Naranjito de Triana, Rubichi (for deep song), and and Chano Lobato (for festive song forms)—will be pure flamenco of the best quality. The same applies to Fosforito, now retired, and Terremoto, who died in 1981, but both worked recently enough for their singing to be digitally recorded. Enrique Morente and Carmen Linares are great singers who experiment with styles and with instrumental accompaniment. José Mercé stands in between: he has been, and is trying to be again, one of the purest and most powerful, the one whom most of the younger generation of Gypsies admire. I am told by reliable flamencos that once a singer has played with fusion, he can never get back to the real thing. I hope they are wrong in his case.

There are many others who are to my taste: Rancapino and José Vargas El Mono for the festive styles, Joaquín El Zambo for the Jerez-style bulerías, and Aurora Vargas and Tomasa La Macanita for their voices, not to mention the many who can excel when not showing their drug problem. But others, at least as experienced as I, might give a quite different list.

Note that few, if any, singers master all styles. Thus, if you want tarantas you must listen to a singer from eastern Andalusia; Carmen Linares is among the very best. Likewise, I have heard the jaberas of Málaga massacred to the point of being unrecognizable by such great singers as Chocolate (from Seville) and the late Camarón (from Cádiz).

Guitarists

The list is, if anything, even longer. Paco de Lucía stands alone and has influenced most others alive today, though he no longer plays much flamenco. In his case, whatever he plays—flamenco, a sort of jazz, or classical (his recording of the Rodrigo guitar concerto is one of the best)—he is spellbindingly good: a virtuoso with artistic integrity. Manolo Sanlúcar is also an iconic figure. These two play together in Carlos Saura's *Sevillanas,* a unique occurrence.

Most of the best guitarists are accompanists, since solo guitar was until recently better known outside Spain than in. But today Paco Peña continues to play solo that would be approved by any flamenco, however traditional, while soloists such as Gerardo Nuñez and Vicente Amigo are popular virtuosos who are taking flamenco away from its roots, though both are good flamencos.

Of the accompanists, the Habichuela brothers of Granada are still at the top in the Granadan style, with the Cortés brothers (Paco and Miguel Angel) close to it; in Madrid, Pedro Sierra, originally from Barcelona, is among the best; in and around Seville, Manolo Franco, Enrique El Melchor, and many others are at the top of their profession; and of the Jerez legacy, Moraíto is supreme, but many others are excellent, not least Diego del Morao, Moraíto's son (and great nephew of the legendary Morao). Every year, more new players astonish by their gifts, and I have no doubt this list does injustice to many.

Magazines

Apart from *Alma 100,* for which I give the data in appendix 4, every country has its magazines, many more or less short-lived.

United States: *Flamenco: The Journal of Flamenco Artistry,* 943 Fifth Street, Suite 6, Santa Monica, CA 90403, tel.: (310) 394-2317, fax: (390) 458-3120. There are others, no doubt.

United Kingdom: *Flamenco International,* P.O. Box 15085, London N8 7WD, tel. 020-8348-3777, fax 020-8348-0562.

Bibliography

Germany: *Anda! Zeitschrift für Flamenco*, Rothenberg 41, 48143 Münster, tel. 02514-827.828, fax 827.829, URL www.anda.de/flamenco, e-mail flamenco@anda.de.

Netherlands: *Revista Aficionao*, Apothekersdijk 4, 2312 DC Leiden, tel. 71.51.48.158, e-mail marlies@xsforall.nl.

Spain: *La Caña*, calle Utrillas 6 bajo A, 28043 Madrid, tel. 91-338.9191; *El Olivo*, subscriptions to Roque Larea Carmona, plaza de Andalucía 1, 23730 Villanueva de la Reina, (Jaen), tel. 953-537.110, fax 953-756.799; and *Candil*, calle Maestra 11, Apto de correos 510, 23011 (Jaen).

Appendix 4
SOURCES AND ADDRESSES

A good source of information is the monthly magazine *Alma 100*, which gives a dozen pages or so of addresses (physical or electronic) of what is happening throughout Spain, and where and when. This includes dance courses. From abroad you would have to subscribe by International Postal Giro to *Alma 100*, calle Duque de Alba 3, 2º-A, 28012 Madrid. A six-month subscription is currently 21 Euros from Europe and 33 Euros from the rest of the world. You can check this by telephone or fax, +34-91-420.43.33, or by e-mail, alma100@ teleline.es. This is a new magazine, and I hope it succeeds, for I know no other source of information as complete (except Gamboa's 450-page companion, listed in the bibliography).

The last few years have seen an explosion of flamenco Web sites. Some of them are (inevitably) fairly tacky. But the first of them, www.flamenco-world.com, seems to be good and is in English as well as Spanish. For Spanish speakers, the Web site of the Centro Andaluz de Flamenco (http://caf.cica.es) has an online magazine called *Alboreá*.

The only foundation for flamenco studies is the Centro Andaluz de Flamenco (CAF), Plaza San Juan, 1, 11403 Jerez-de-la-Frontera, Cádiz, tel. +34-956-34.92. 65, fax 32.11.27, e-mail atenorio@cica.es (for librarian Ana Tenorio), Web site http://caf.cica.es. The foundation has a large collection of videos in constant use. They can give information on festivals, dance courses, peñas, and the like.

The company Manual Marao and Gitanos de Jerez have had the excellent idea of helping tourists to understand flamenco via their Web site www.gitanosde-jerez.com, which they put in English as well as in Spanish. It is multimedia, with pictures, videos, and music.

The main sources of good flamenco are the flamenco festivals, which are on the increase, and the peñas, where performances are commonly, though not always, on Saturday nights.

Seville

FESTIVAL Taking place in early October on alternate years, the Bienal competition is one of the two major events and is interlaced with shows and performances. The date varies, but you can get information via either the Instituto Cervantes in your country, or the Seville Tourist Office, or the CAF in Jerez.

PEÑAS El Chozas, calle Ricardo Palma, 133; Torres Macarena, calle Torrijiano, 29; La Fragua, calle Caldereros, 30, Bellavista suburb. In the center, the Tablao de Curro Vélez, calle Rodó, used to give quality performances when I knew it in the early 1990s.

Jerez

FESTIVAL Four months before it starts, usually in late February or early March, it has been receiving 125 applications for dance courses per week from twenty different countries. See the information for the Centro Andaluz de Flamenco. This festival, apart from the dance courses, offers everything from major theater spectacles, to recitals, to performances in the peñas and lectures. To take it all in—up to three performances a night—would require more stamina than I can command. And for those also following dance classes by day, heroism.

PEÑAS There are twelve or thirteen of these, all of which welcome strangers. Addresses can be obtained via the Tourist Office. There are also three or four dance academies, operating throughout the year. (Contact CAF.)

Córdoba

FESTIVAL This is the other big competition, again with performances, as in the Seville Bienal. Here the emphasis is more on guitar (it was started by the great Cordoban guitarist Paco Peña) and on dance, for which there are several prize categories. The guitar festival is held in early July; the dance festival is in early May, coinciding with the May celebrations, which include a competition for the best patio. Flowers galore.

Peñas There are several, though I don't know if they welcome strangers. The Peña Fosforito is active, as is the Peña Flamenca de Córdoba in calle Romero Barrios. Try through the Tourist Office.

Granada

There is no flamenco festival, but during the summer festival of classical music (June–July) there are *trasnoches*—flamenco performances after the classical concerts, starting at midnight and lasting through the wee hours.

From September to June, the Teatro Alhambra has one day per week dedicated to flamenco. In winter, the Peña La Platería has performances on Thursday and Saturday nights. If you have a car, the Parra Flamenca in Huétor Vega, up in the hills, has Saturday night performances.

There is a school for flamenco and Spanish owned by Nacho Martín: Carmen de las Cuevas, Cuesta de los Chinos, 15, 18010 Granada, tel. 958-221062, fax 958-220.476, Web site www.carmencuevas.com, e-mail info@carmencuevas.com. (They find lodging for students.)

Madrid

Festival Held in March; much of it is well advertised and in theaters.

Peñas The capital is not the easiest place to find real flamenco. It is there, but you need to spend time there to know where. In a metropolis, the "in" places change, especially when the general public gets to know of them. Thus I recommend La Soleá, calle Cava Baja, 34, in the knowledge that this may well destroy it. The Tourist Office will point you firmly to the tourist tablaos, some of which can be good—La Casa Patas, for example, and possibly the Peña Duende.

Many of the smaller towns have festivals, with Linares and La Unión specializing in the eastern songs such as the taranta, and every town, small or large, has at least one peña, even those on the tourist-ridden Costa del Sol.

Appendix 5
COMPACT DISC CONTENTS

Disc mastered by Jonathan Tam, Charterhouse Recording Studio.

Track	Performers	Source	Play time
1. Toná	Dolores Agujeta By kind permission of the artist.	Promotional CD	2'37"
2. Siguiriya 1	Chocolate and Diego Amaya By kind permission of Manuel Morao and Gitanos de Jerez.	Evocación de Terremoto	2'11" (extract)
3. Siguiriya 2	Antonio El Monea	Recorded by the author	1'49"
4. Soleá 1	José Menese and Melchor de Marchena By permission of BMG Music, Spain.	"Cantes Flamencos Básicos"	7'32"
5. Soleá 2	David Lagos and Alfredo Lagos	Private recording	5'22"
6. Bulería	Melchora Ortega and Pascual de Lorca	Private recording	5'47" (extract)

Appendix 5

Track	Performers	Source	Play time
7. Tiento-tango	María del M. Fernández	Recorded by the author	4'21" (extract)
8. Alegrías	Chano Lobato and Luis Moneo	"De Jerez a los puertos"	3'22" (extract)
	By kind permission of Manuel Morao and Gitanos de Jerez.		
9. Peteneras	Juan Zarzuela and Pedro Pimentel	Recorded by the author	3'05"
10. Fandango local	Elisa La del Horno and Rafael Hoces	Recorded by the author	4'13"
11. Fandango grande	Antonio El Monea	Recorded by the author	0'50"
12. Malagueña	Dolores Agujeta and Agujetas Chico	Promotional CD	3'05"
	By kind permission of the artists.		
13. Rondeña	Juan Zarzuela and Pedro Pimentel	Recorded by the author	2'03"
14. Media granaína	Mercedes Hidalgo and Miguel Ochando	Recorded by the author	4'37" (extract)
15. Granaína	El Colorao and El Coquillo	Recorded by the author	3'19" (extract)

Compact Disc Contents

Track	Performers	Source	Play time
16. Taranta	Juan Cortés Coquillo, guitar solo	Recorded by the author	4'11"
17. Taranto	Juan Pinilla and Carlos Zárate	Recorded by the author	2'27"
18. Farruca	Juan Pinilla and Carlos Zárate	Recorded by the author	3'21"
19. Garrotín	Lola La Cartujana and Carlos Zárate	Recorded by the author	3'00"
20. Guajira	Sensi and Carlos Zárate	Recorded by the author	4'39"
21. Saeta	Singer unknown	Recorded by the author	3'46"

INDEX

Page numbers in italics refer to illustrations.

Index